Alex Troup is a barrister who practises from St. John's Chambers, Bristol. He specialises in the law of succession, trusts and Court of Protection matters, and is ranked as a "star individual" for chancery matters in Chambers UK. He also has a busy practice as a mediator and is on the panel of approved mediators for the Court of Protection Mediation Scheme.

A Practical Guide to the Law of Statutory Wills

A Practical Guide to the Law of Statutory Wills

Alex Troup
Barrister and Mediator
MA (Oxon), TEP

Law Brief Publishing

Published 2021 by Law Brief Publishing, an imprint of Law Brief Publishing Ltd
30 The Parks
Minehead
Somerset
TA24 8BT

www.lawbriefpublishing.com

Paperback: 978-1-913715-72-4

To my parents, who always act in my best interests.

And to my wife Jane, for everything.

CONTENTS

INTRODUCTION

The aim of this book is to provide the reader with a practical guide to the law of statutory wills.

What is a statutory will?

A statutory will is a will (or codicil) executed by a third party with the authority of the Court of Protection on behalf of an adult person who lacks capacity to make a will himself or herself. Such a will is known as a statutory will because it is made pursuant to statute – namely the Mental Capacity Act 2005. Section 18(1)(i) of that Act specifically provides that the Court of Protection's powers as respects P's property and affairs extend to "*the execution for P of a will*". The execution of a statutory will for P is a decision which must be made by the Court of Protection, and cannot be entrusted to a deputy or an attorney under a Lasting Power of Attorney.[1]

Terminology

This is a practical guide. Its aim is to provide clear and practical assistance for anyone (whether lawyer or layman) who is considering making or finds themselves involved in a statutory will application. Every attempt has been made to avoid technical jargon and lengthy discussions of points of academic interest (although the footnotes will provide suggestions for further reading for anyone who is interested). However the following terms have been used throughout the book and should be explained at the outset:

"MCA 2005" – This refers to the Mental Capacity Act 2005, which provides the statutory framework for any statutory will application. The Mental Capacity Act 2005 is freely available online.[2]

---

[1] See s.20(3)(b) of the MCA 2005 and *In re P (Statutory Will)* [2010] Ch 33 at para 30.

[2] https://www.legislation.gov.uk/ukpga/2005/9/contents

"The Code of Practice" – This refers to the Code of Practice which accompanies the MCA 2005 and provides guidance and information about how the MCA 2005 works in practice. The Code of Practice is also freely available online.[3]

"P" – This is the person on whose behalf the statutory will is authorised. The same abbreviation is used in both the MCA 2005 and the Court of Protection Rules 2017.[4] When referring to P in this book the masculine pronouns "he/him" are used simply for convenience, but in each case they should be deemed to include reference to "she/her".

"Testamentary capacity" – This refers to a person's capacity to make a will or codicil.

The arrangement of this book

It is suggested that anyone considering or involved in a statutory will application should approach their particular case in a structured way by asking the following questions, which reflect the arrangement of the chapters in this book.

1. **Is P an adult who lacks testamentary capacity?** This fundamental question is addressed in **Chapter 1**. If P is a child, or is an adult who *has* capacity to make a will, then the reader can put this book down now. The Court of Protection will have no jurisdiction to authorise a statutory will in such a case.

2. **Does P currently have a will?** In order to decide whether it is appropriate to apply for a statutory will, you will need to know whether P currently has a will (and if so what it says) or, if P does not

[3] https://www.gov.uk/government/publications/mental-capacity-act-code-of-practice

[4] See rule 2.1 of the Court of Protection rules 2017 which define P as "*any person… who lacks or, so far as consistent with the context, is alleged to lack capacity to make a decision or decisions in relation to any matter that is the subject of an application to the court…*".

have a will, how P's estate will be distributed if P dies intestate. These issues are addressed in **Chapter 2**.

3. **Would it be in P's best interests for a statutory will to be executed on his behalf and, if so, on what terms?** The Court of Protection will only authorise the execution of a statutory will if it is in P's bests interests to do so. Likewise, P's best interests will determine the terms of any statutory will. P's bests interests are therefore critical to any statutory will application, and they are discussed in **Chapter 3**.

4. **When should an application for a statutory will be made?** Whilst there is in theory no limit to the circumstances in which the Court of Protection will authorise a statutory will, there are certain scenarios which commonly arise in practice where the Court of Protection is likely to authorise a statutory will. Those scenarios are set out in **Chapter 4**, which also contains a discussion of the case law which has developed in relation to each of those scenarios.

5. **Does your case involve an international element?** This may arise where P owns property abroad, where P is domiciled abroad, or where a statutory will (or equivalent) has been authorised on P's behalf by a foreign court. These scenarios are discussed in **Chapter 5**.

6. **What procedure should be followed when applying for a statutory will?** This is explained in **Chapter 6**.

7. **How do I make an urgent application for a statutory will in a medical emergency?** If P dies then the Court of Protection no longer has jurisdiction to authorise a statutory will on P's behalf. Accordingly if there is a risk that P may die imminently, it may be necessary to apply for a statutory will as a matter of urgency. This difficult situation is addressed in **Chapter 7**.

8. **Who will pay the costs of a statutory will application?** It is not unusual for the parties to a statutory will application to incur substantial legal costs. The important question of who will ultimately bear those costs is discussed in **Chapter 8**.

9. **What is the nature and effect of a statutory will?** This is addressed in **Chapter 9**.

10. **Can I negotiate a compromise of a statutory will application out of court?** The answer is yes, although any compromise will need to be approved by, and given effect to by an order of, the Court of Protection. Mediation is becoming an increasingly popular means of resolving statutory will applications, and there is a Court of Protection Mediation Pilot Scheme through which mediations can be arranged. This is discussed in **Chapter 10**.

Caselaw

Throughout this book reference will be made to the relevant caselaw. Most of this can be found for free online at www.bailii.org, which is the website of the British and Irish Legal Information Institute. Its Case Law Search function includes the ability to search cases decided by the England and Wales Court of Protection. Many of the cases are also reported in the Court of Protection Law Reports (COPLR) which are published by LexisNexis UK.

Further reading

Any reader who wishes to explore the topic of statutory wills in more depth, or to explore other aspects of the law of wills or the Court of Protection, is referred to the following textbooks by way of further reading:

1. Heywood and Massey: Court of Protection Practice (loose-leaf) edited by David Rees

2. Court of Protection Practice 2021 edited by Gordon R. Ashton

3. Court of Protection Handbook: A User's Guide (3rd ed.) by Alex Ruck Keene, Kate Edwards, Anselm Eldergill & Sophie Miles

4. Williams on Wills (10th ed.) by Francis Barlow, Richard Wallington, Susannah Meadway & James MacDougald.

5. Theobald on Wills (19th ed.) by Alexander Learmonth, Charlotte Ford, Thomas Fletcher, Master Clark and Master Shuman.
6. The Mental Capacity Casebook by Dr Tracey Ryan-Morgan.

39 Essex Street Chambers produce a Mental Capacity Report on a monthly basis which is freely available via their website: https://www.39essex.com/resources-and-training/mental-capacity-law/

A word of warning

Finally, a word of warning. The law on statutory wills is technical and complex. There is no substitute for experience in this area. This book provides guidance on the general law but should not be treated as advice in relation to any particular case. It is strongly recommended that any lay person who finds themselves involved in a statutory will case should seek specialist legal advice.

The law is stated as at 1st May 2021.

CHAPTER ONE

IS P AN ADULT WHO LACKS TESTAMENTARY CAPACITY?

There are two fundamental requirements which must be satisfied before the Court of Protection can authorise a statutory will for P. The first is that P must be an adult. The second is that P must lack testamentary capacity.

P must be an adult

P must be an adult aged 18 or over.[5] The Court of Protection cannot authorise a statutory will for a child. This limitation is not surprising, because there is a general prohibition on anybody under the age of 18 making a will, even if they have no cognitive impairment.[6] There is one reported case where the Court of Protection was prepared to authorise the creation of a trust (as opposed to a statutory will) in order to prevent the assets of P, who was under 18, passing on intestacy to his parents, but the facts of that case were exceptional and it should not be assumed that the Court would proceed in this way in every case where P is a child.[7]

P must lack testamentary capacity

If P *has* testamentary capacity, then the Court of Protection will have no power to authorise a statutory will. Instead in that scenario it will be up to P himself to decide whether or not to make a will and, if so, in what terms. It is only if P *lacks* testamentary capacity that the Court of Protection will have power to authorise a statutory will.

---

[5] See s.18(2) of the MCA 2005.

[6] See s.7 of the Wills Act 1837. There is an exception for privileged testators such as soldiers in actual military service or seamen at sea: see generally Theobald on Wills (19th ed.) at paras 3-040 onwards.

[7] *Re CJF; LCN v. KF, AH, EH and CJF* [2019] EWCOP 1.

It is up to the person applying for the statutory will to produce suitable evidence to prove that P lacks testamentary capacity. That evidence usually takes the form of a capacity assessment carried out by an appropriately qualified medical practitioner or other professional which is recorded on Form COP3.[8] In many cases that capacity assessment is not disputed and the Court of Protection accepts it at face value. But there are cases where the evidence is disputed, typically because it is alleged that the assessor has ignored one of the principles set out in s.1 of the MCA 2004, has applied the wrong legal test, or has carried out the assessment incorrectly.

Who can assess capacity?

It is not only doctors who can assess P's testamentary capacity. Any practitioner who has appropriate expertise so as to allow them to apply the legal test may carry out an assessment. Suitable candidates might include an approved mental health professional, a social worker[9], a psychologist, a nurse, a speech therapist or an occupational therapist.[10]

How to instruct the assessor

The instructions to the doctor or other professional person carrying out the assessment should generally take the form of a letter which addresses the following issues:

(1) P's family background and personal circumstances.

(2) P's financial position.

(3) Any orders which have previously been made by the Court of Protection in relation to P, including in particular whether the court has made an order appointing a deputy to manage P's property and affairs.

---

[8] Form COP3 is discussed in Chapter 6 of this book.

[9] See *A Local Authority v. SY* [2013] EWHC 3485 (COP) at para 22.

[10] See the list of suggested practitioners in the guidance notes on Form COP3.

(4) The terms of any previous wills or codicils made by P.

(5) The relevant principles set out in section 1 of the MCA 2005, as discussed below.

(6) The legal test for testamentary capacity as set out in sections 2 and 3 of the MCA 2005 and the relevant information set out in *Banks v. Goodfellow* (1870) LR 5 QB 549, as discussed below.

(7) The assessor should be told that if they are unclear about any aspect of their instructions then they should ask for clarification.

How the assessor should carry out the assessment

STEP 1 – Consider the relevant principles in section 1 of the MCA 2005

The first step in carrying out any assessment of P's testamentary capacity is for the assessor to consider the relevant principles set out in section 1 of the MCA 2005. Section 1 sets out five key principles but only three of them are relevant to capacity assessments. The three relevant principles are as follows:

> "*1. The Principles*
>
> *(1) The following principles apply for the purposes of this Act.*
>
> *(2) A person must be assumed to have capacity unless it is established that he lacks capacity.*
>
> *(3) A person is not to be treated as unable to make a decision unless all practicable steps to help him to do so have been taken without success.*
>
> (4) *A person is not to be treated as unable to make a decision merely because he makes an unwise decision…*"

The **first principle** set out in section 1(2) contains the so-called presumption of capacity. The effect of this presumption is that the Court of Protection will proceed on the assumption that P has testamentary capacity unless the person applying for the statutory will proves otherwise. In a recent case this presumption was described as the paramount principle in the MCA 2005.[11] The existence of this presumption is why the onus lies on the applicant to produce sufficient evidence to persuade the Court that P lacks testamentary capacity. The civil standard of proof applies, and so the applicant must satisfy the court on the balance of probabilities – or in other words, that it is more likely than not – that P lacks testamentary capacity.[12]

The **second principle** set out in section 1(3) contemplates that P may need support in order to make a will. The fact that P needs such support does not mean that he lacks testamentary capacity. Quite the reverse: the effect of section 1(3) is that if P is able to satisfy the test in sections 2 and 3 of the MCA 2005 with suitable support then he will have testamentary capacity. In such a scenario P should be given the appropriate support so that he can make a will himself. Anyone applying for a statutory will must therefore prove that all practicable steps to help P make a will have been taken without success before the Court will be prepared to decide that P lacks capacity.

Chapter 3 of the Code of Practice provides practical guidance on how to support people to make decisions for themselves. Anybody carrying out a capacity assessment should refer to the guidance. The guidance includes suggestions about how to provide all the relevant information to P, how to communicate with P in an appropriate way (such as visual aids or non-verbal communication), how to make P feel at ease (such as by conducting the capacity test in a familiar location or at a particular time of day) and how to support P to make the decision (such as by asking a third party to help or support P to make choices or express a view).

---

[11] See *Tower Hamlets LBC v. PB* [2020] 4 WLR 94 at para 51(iv).

[12] See s.2(4) of the MCA 2005.

Example

Neil has a diagnosis of secondary progressive multiple sclerosis which has progressed to the point of extreme physical debilitation. A solicitor attends on Neil who, with the assistance of a colleague and a doctor, takes instructions by putting questions to Neil. Neil answers yes or no by either nodding or shaking his head. He gives more detailed answers via a spelling board and blinking. The fact that Neil requires such support does not mean that he lacks testamentary capacity.[13]

There can be a fine line between a person supporting P to make a will and that person exercising undue influence over P in order to procure a will in his or her favour.[14] If the boundary is crossed then the will in question will be invalid.[15] If any person carrying out a mental capacity assessment considers that P may be subject to undue influence then that person should seek legal advice before proceeding any further.

The **third principle** set out in section 1(4) is that P should not be treated as lacking capacity merely because he makes an unwise decision.[16] This has particular resonance in relation to wills, since the Courts have repeatedly emphasised that a person is free to make a will which is unfair or spiteful. This point was emphasised by the Court of Appeal in *Gill v. RSPCA* [2011] Ch 380 where Lord Neuberger stated:

---

[13] This example is loosely based on the case of *Sharp v. Adam* [2006] EWCA Civ 449, although on the facts it was held that the testator lacked testamentary capacity.

[14] The court was alive to this possibility in the case of *In the matter of Ann Clarke* [2012] EWHC 2257 (COP) where Peter Jackson J stated at para 36: "*…I cannot exclude the possibility that [the applicant] exerts influence on [P], but I do not find that this currently invalidates her general testamentary capacity. Whether any particular will that she may make could subsequently be challenged is not a matter for this court at this time*".

[15] The law on undue influence as it applies to wills was helpfully summarised by Lewison J (as he then was) in *Re Edwards* [2007] EWHC 119 (Ch) at para 47.

[16] See *A, B and C v. X and Z* [2013] COPLR 1 at para 34 where Hedley J stated that it is important "*to bear in mind that an eccentric disposition of property is not itself evidence of incapacity by reason of s 1(4)*".

> *"Subject to statutes such as the Inheritance (Provision for Family and Dependants) Act 1975, the law in this country permits people to leave their assets as they see fit, and experience of human nature generally, and of wills in particular, demonstrates that peoples' wishes can be unexpected, inexplicable, unfair, and even improper. As I have mentioned, a court should be very slow to find that a will does not represent the genuine wishes of the testatrix simply because its terms are surprising, inconsistent with what she said during her lifetime, unfair, or even vindictive or perverse."*

Having said this, if P proposes to make a will in terms which are surprising, then that is a material factor which any person assessing P's testamentary capacity may legitimately take into account.[17]

STEP 2 – The assessor must apply the correct legal test

Having considered the relevant principles discussed above, the next stage is for the person carrying out the assessment to apply to correct legal test for testamentary capacity. The legal test for determining whether P has testamentary capacity is set out in sections 2 and 3 of the MCA 2005.[18] Insofar as they are relevant, those sections provide as follows:

> "***2. People who lack capacity***
>
> *(1) For the purposes of this Act, a person lacks capacity in relation to a matter if at the material time he is unable to make a decision for himself in relation to the matter because of an impairment of, or a disturbance in the functioning of, the mind or brain.*

[17] See, for example, *Sharp v. Adam* [[2006] EWCA Civ 449, where the fact that the testator had excluded his daughters as beneficiaries was a key factor in the court's decision that the will in question was invalid.

[18] The MCA 2005 is the appropriate test to apply in the context of a statutory will application. Where a dispute arises after P's death as to whether P had capacity to make a will, then the authorities suggest that in that context the court will apply the common law test in *Banks v. Goodfellow* (1870) LR 5 QB 549 instead of the statutory test under the MCA 2005: see *Clitheroe v. Bond* [2021] EWHC 1102 (Ch).

(2) It does not matter whether impairment or disturbance is permanent or temporary.

(3) A lack of capacity cannot be established merely by reference to –

(a) a person's age or appearance, or

(b) a condition of his, or an aspect of his behaviour, which might lead others to make unjustified assumptions about his capacity.

(4) In proceedings under this Act or any other enactment, any question whether a person lacks capacity within the meaning of this Act must be decided on the balance of probabilities…"

3. Inability to make decisions

(1) For the purposes of section 2, a person is unable to make a decision for himself if he is unable –

(a) To understand the information relevant to the decision,

(b) To retain that information,

(c) To use or weigh that information as part of the process of making the decision, or

(d) To communicate his decision (whether by talking, using sign language or any other means).

(2) A person is not to be regarded as unable to understand the information relevant to a decision if he is able to understand an explanation of it given to him in a way that is appropriate to his circumstances (using simple language, visual aids or any other means).

(3) The fact that a person is able to retain the information relevant to a decision for a short period only does not prevent him from being regarded as able to make the decision.

(4) The information relevant to a decision includes information about the reasonably foreseeable consequences of –
(a) deciding one way or another, or

(b) *failing to make the decision.*"

It is clear from the opening words of section 2(1) that the test is whether P has capacity to make a decision in relation to a particular matter – which in the context of this book means the decision to make a will – and at a particular time. In other words, the test is decision-specific and time-specific. It follows that it is quite possible for P to have capacity to make a will but nevertheless to lack capacity to make decisions in relation to other matters. Likewise, it is possible that P may have testamentary capacity on one day but lack capacity on the next day – or indeed that P may have testamentary capacity at one particular time of day but lack testamentary capacity later that same day.

These possibilities are well illustrated by the case of *A, B and C v. X and Z* [2013] COPLR 1, where it was held that whilst X lacked capacity to manage his own affairs and to conduct litigation, he nevertheless had a qualified capacity to make a will. The Judge stated at para 36:

> "*In the event, I have concluded that I cannot make a general declaration that X lacks testamentary capacity, but that needs to be strongly qualified. There will undoubtedly be times when he does lack testamentary capacity. There will be many times when he does not do so. The times when he does lack such capacity are likely to become more frequent. It follow that, in my judgment, any will now made by X, if unaccompanied by contemporary medical evidence asserting capacity, may be seriously open to challenge...*"

The test set out in section 2(1) of the MCA 2005 involves three separate stages which anyone carrying out a capacity assessment needs to consider in turn and in the following order.[19]

[19] This approach is based upon *PC v. City of York Council* [2013] COPLR 409 where the first instance judge's capacity assessment was overturned on appeal because he had considered the diagnostic test (stage 2) before the functional test (stage 1), which led him to watering down the causative nexus between those two stages (stage 3). Interestingly, the Code of Practice suggests approaching matters in the same order as the first instance judge. However, in the later case of *Norfolk CC v. PB* [2015] COPLR 118 it was held (at para 89) that the decision in *PC v. City of York Council* did not lay down a different test or take the questions in reverse order: it merely

The **first stage** is to determine whether P is unable to make a decision for himself in relation to the matter. In the context of this book, the matter in question is the making of a will. This is known as the functional test. It is expanded upon by section 3(1) of the MCA 2005 which explains that a person will be unable to make a decision for himself if he is unable to understand "the information relevant to the decision", to retain that information, to use or weigh that information as part of the process of making the decision and to communicate his decision.

In the context of statutory wills, the "information relevant to the decision" is that set out in the old case of *Banks v. Goodfellow* (1870) LR 5 QB 549 where it was held that:

> "*It is essential to the exercise of such a power that a testator shall understand the nature of the act and its effects; shall understand the extent of the property of which he is disposing; shall be able to comprehend and appreciate the claims to which he ought to give effect; and with a view to the latter object, that no disorder of the mind shall poison his affections, pervert his sense of right, or prevent the exercise of his natural faculties – that no insane delusion shall influence his will in disposing of his property and bring about a disposal of it which, if the mind had been sound, would not have been made.*" (emphasis supplied)

This is supplemented by section 3(4) of the MCA 2005, which provides that "the information relevant to the decision" also includes the information about the reasonably foreseeable consequences of deciding one way or another, or failing to make the decision.

The upshot of all of this is that the information which P must be able to understand, to retain and to use or weigh as part of the process of making a decision is as follows:

---

stressed the importance of establishing the causal connection between the first two stages. Despite that indication, it is thought to be helpful to analyse matters in the same order as is set out in *PC v. City of York Council*, which reflects the order set out in s.2(1) of the MCA 2005.

(1) the nature of a will and its effects;

(2) the extent of his property;

(3) the claims to which he ought to give effect;

(4) the reasonably foreseeable consequences of making, or not making, a will.[20]

The courts have repeatedly emphasised that the test for capacity is not to be equated with a memory test.[21] So the mere fact that P cannot remember the terms of a previous will[22], or the value of his property[23], does not of itself mean that he lacks testamentary capacity, so long as he is capable of accessing the information.

The information set out above should be explained to P in a way that is appropriate to his circumstances, as required by section 3(2), before the capacity assessment is then carried out.[24] Chapter 3 of the Code of Conduct provides practical guidance on how this should be done.

The **second stage** is to determine whether there is an impairment of, or a disturbance in the functioning of, P's mind or brain. This is a medical issue, and is known as the diagnostic test. There is no limit placed on the range of impairments, or disturbances in the functioning of the brain, which will satisfy this requirement, and section 2(2) specifically provides that it does not matter whether the impairment or disturbance is temporary or permanent.

The **third stage** is to establish that P's inability to make a will is caused by the impairment, or a disturbance in the functioning of, his mind or

---

[20] In *Simon v. Byford* [2014] EWCA Civ 280 one of the foreseeable consequences of the testatrix leaving her shareholding in family company to her 4 children in equal shares was that the company may end up in deadlock.

[21] See *Simon v. Byford*, above, at para 40.

[22] As was the case in *Simon v. Byford*, above.

[23] See *Schrader v. Schrader* [2013] EWHC 466 (Ch) at para 41.

[24] See para 4.16 of the Code of Conduct and *AMDC v. AG* [2020] 4 WLR 166 at para 24(a).

brain. In other words, it is necessary to establish a causal link between Step 1 and Step 2. If P is unable to make his will due to a reason other than an impairment or disturbance in the function of his mind or brain, then he will not lack capacity.

It follows that the test for determining whether P has testamentary capacity to make a will is not just a medical issue. The diagnostic test (step 2) is only one element of the test, and any assessment must also consider the functional test and the causal test. That is why it is not just doctors who can carry out a capacity assessment.

STEP 3 – How to deal with problem areas

There are three particular problem areas which commonly arise in practice.

Fluctuating capacity – It is not uncommon to encounter cases where P's testamentary fluctuates. For instance, it is notorious that a person with a diagnosis of dementia may have good days and bad days. His capacity may even fluctuate over the course of a single day, so that he may have capacity in the morning but not in the afternoon. In such cases the assessment should be carried out on a date and at a time when P's capacity is likely to be at its highest, so as to comply with fundamental principle set out in section 1(3) of the MCA 2005, as discussed above.

Likewise, it is critical in such cases that the capacity assessment is based upon a contemporaneous meeting with P rather than upon historic notes, and that a written record of the assessment is kept so that it can be produced if the assessment is challenged at any stage in the future.[25]

This is in keeping with the so-called Golden Rule, which states that when a solicitor is instructed to prepare a will for an aged testator, or for one who has been seriously ill, he should arrange for a medical practitioner first to satisfy himself as to the capacity and understanding of the testator, and to make a contemporaneous record of his examination and

---

[25] See *A, B and C v. X and Z* [2013] COPLR 1 at para 36, which is quoted above in the discussion of the legal test for testamentary capacity.

findings.[26] This is a rule of good practice for solicitors rather than a touchstone of the validity of the will, and there may be cases where it is not practical to follow it.[27] If it is followed, however, then it should minimise the risk of disputes arising in future as to the validity of the will in question.

Refusal by P to undergo a capacity assessment – There are cases where P simply refuses to undergo a capacity assessment and refuses to consent to disclosure of his or her medical records. It is legitimate to seek to persuade P to undergo an assessment, for example by carefully explaining the purpose of the assessment to P or by giving P a choice of who will carry out the assessment. If there are reasonable grounds to believe that P's refusal is due to the undue influence of a third party, it may be possible to invoke the inherent jurisdiction of the High Court.[28] Ultimately, however, P cannot be compelled to do so against their will. The absence of a capacity assessment is not a bar to the court making a finding of lack of capacity, but in such cases the court will be cautious before concluding that the presumption of capacity in s.1(2) of the MCA 2005 has been rebutted.[29] The court may simply have to do the best it can on such other evidence as may be available. That evidence could include P's own conduct if P attends court[30], any documents written by P, videos of P, and evidence from P's family members and associates.

An applicant faced with this situation may issue an application for a statutory will but should file a witness statement explaining why he has not been able to obtain a capacity assessment, what attempts (if any) he

[26] See *Key v. Key* [2010] 1 WLR 2020.

[27] For instance, *Goss-Custard v. Templeman* [2020] EWHC 632 (Ch) at paras 115.

[28] See the discussion of the inherent jurisdiction in *Croydon LBC v KR* [2019] EWHC 2498 (Fam); [2020] COPLR 285, at paras 31 onwards.

[29] *Baker Tilly (a firm) v. Makar* [2013] EWHC 759 (Ch); [2013] COPLR 245; [2013] 3 Costs LR 444.

[30] See the *Baker Tilly* case, above, where the High Court cautioned against concluding that a litigant in person lacked litigation capacity on the basis of the litigant's erratic behaviour in and outside Court; and *Re RGS* [2012] EWHC 4162 (COP).

has made to obtain a capacity assessment, and why he knows or believes that P lacks capacity to make a will.[31]

Remote assessments – There are occasions when face-to-face capacity assessments are simply not possible. In such a scenario a capacity assessment may be carried out remotely over platforms such as Zoom, Teams, Facetime or Skype. Such remote capacity assessments have become common during the COVID-19 pandemic. There is no doubt that such remote assessments are lawful[32], although they require careful preparation and creativity to overcome the challenges which they present.

STEP 4 – Follow the guidance given by the Court of Protection

In the case of *AMDC v. AG and CI*[33], the Court of Protection gave the following guidance to any expert providing a written report to the court on P's capacity. It is suggested that this guidance should be followed (or at least carefully considered) by anyone carrying out a capacity assessment:

(1) An expert report on capacity is not a clinical assessment but should seek to assist the court to determine certain identified issues. The expert should therefore pay close regard to (i) the terms of the Mental Capacity Act and Code of Practice, and (ii) the letter of instruction.

(2) The letter of instruction should identify the decisions under consideration, the relevant information for each decision, the need to consider the diagnostic and functional elements of capacity, and the causal relationship between any impairment and the inability to decide. It will assist the court if the expert structures their report accordingly. If an expert witness is unsure what decisions they are being asked to consider, what the relevant information is in respect to those decisions, or any other matter relevant to the making of their report, they should ask for clarification.

---

31 Practice Direction 9A, para 14.

32 *BP v. Surrey* [2020] EWCOP 17.

33 *AMDC v. AG and CI* [2020] EWCOP 58.

(3) It is important that the parties and the court can see from their reports that the expert has understood and applied the presumption of capacity and the other fundamental principles set out at section 1 of the MCA 2005.

(4) In cases where the expert assesses capacity in relation to more than one decision, (i) broad-brush conclusions are unlikely to be as helpful as specific conclusions as to the capacity to make each decision; (ii) experts should ensure that their opinions in relation to each decision are consistent and coherent.

(5) An expert report should not only state the expert's opinions, but also explain the basis of each opinion. The court is unlikely to give weight to an opinion unless it knows on what evidence it was based, and what reasoning led to it being formed.

(6) If an expert changes their opinion on capacity following re-assessment or otherwise, they ought to provide a full explanation of why their conclusion has changed.

(7) The interview with P need not be fully transcribed in the body of the report (although it might be provided in an appendix), but if the expert relies on a particular exchange or something said by P during interview, then at least an account of what was said should be included.

(8) If on assessment P does not engage with the expert, then the expert is not required mechanically to ask P about each and every piece of relevant information if to do so would be obviously futile or even aggravating. However, the report should record what attempts were made to assist P to engage and what alternative strategies were used. If an expert hits a "brick wall" with P then they might want to liaise with others to formulate alternative strategies to engage P. The expert might consider what further bespoke education or support can be given to P to promote P's capacity *or* P's engagement in the decisions which may have to be taken on their behalf. Failure to take steps to assist P to engage and to support her in her decision-making would

be contrary to the fundamental principles of the Mental Capacity Act 2005 ss 1(3) and 3(2).

STEP 5 – What form should a capacity assessment take?

Many capacity assessments are carried out relatively informally and typically take the form of a letter or a short report.

Where the assessment is undertaken in support of a statutory will application to the Court of Protection it should be on Form COP3.[34] Practice Direction 9E states that in addition to the capacity assessment, the evidence in support of a statutory will application should include "an up to date report on P's medical condition, life expectancy and likelihood of requiring increased expenditure in the foreseeable future".[35] It is therefore sensible to ask the person carrying out the capacity assessment to consider these matters in addition to P's testamentary capacity, and to report on them either within the Form COP3 (perhaps using the space for general comments) or in a separate report which can be attached to the Form COP3. The assessor should also be asked to record any relevant wishes and feelings which P is able to express during the assessment, since such wishes and feelings are a relevant factor for the Court of Protection to take into account in determining whether it is in P's best interests to authorise a statutory will and if so in what terms.[36] The court set out guidelines as to how anyone seeking to ascertain P's wishes and feelings should follow in the case of *ADS v. DSM*.[37]

---

[34] Available online at https://www.gov.uk/government/publications/make-a-report-on-someones-capacity -to-make-decisions-form-cop3

[35] See Practice Direction 9E, para 6(p), which requires such information to be included in (or attached as an exhibit to) the witness statement supporting any application for a statutory will.

[36] The best interests test is discussed in Chapter 3 of this book.

[37] [2017] EWCOP 8 at paras 81-82.

If the capacity assessment is being undertaken by an expert pursuant to a direction made by the Court of Protection, the expert's report should comply with the requirements set out in Practice Direction 15A.[38]

Disputes over capacity

Many capacity assessments are uncontroversial, but sometimes they are challenged, either by P himself or herself or by others, such as family members, friends or professionals. In such cases the challenger should as a first step raise the matter with the capacity assessor, and ask them to give reasons for their decision and to provide objective evidence to support it.[39] The challenger might wish to obtain their own capacity assessment.[40] If the dispute cannot be resolved by agreement, then ultimately it will be for the Court of Protection to determine P's capacity, based upon all the evidence. The Court of Protection may give directions to assist it in determining P's capacity in such circumstances, including directing a capacity assessment to be carried out by a single joint expert[41] or by a Court of Protection Visitor.[42]

---

[38] Court of Protection Rules 2017, rule 15.8, and Practice Direction 15A at paras 8 to 12.

[39] The Code of Practice at para 4.63.

[40] The Code of Practice at para 4.65.

[41] Court of Protection Rules 2017, rule 15.12.

[42] See s.49 of the MCA 2005.

CHAPTER TWO

DOES P CURRENTLY HAVE A WILL?

In order to decide whether it is appropriate to apply for a statutory will, you will need to know whether P currently has a will and, if so, what it says. If P does not have a will, you will need to know how P's estate will be distributed under the intestacy rules.

If P *has* capacity to manage his own property and financial affairs then it will be up to P himself to decide whether or not to reveal whether he has made a will and if so what it says.

If P *lacks* capacity to manage his or her own property and financial affairs, then the first step is to find out whether his or her property and affairs are being managed by an attorney under a Lasting Power of Attorney ("LPA") or Enduring Power of Attorney ("EPA") or by a deputy appointed by the Court of Protection. If so it will be up to the attorney or deputy to decide whether it would be in P's best interests to reveal whether P has made a will and if so what it says.

If no attorney or deputy is in place, then it may be in P's best interests to apply for a deputy to be appointed. As part of their duties, any attorney or deputy managing P's property and affairs should obtain a copy of any will made by P and review its terms, not only so that they can avoid acting in a way which unwittingly interferes with P's testamentary intentions[43] but also to decide whether it would be in P's best interests to apply for a statutory will.

---

[43] See *Re Treadwell* [2013] EWHC 2409 (COP); [2013] WTLR WTLR 1445, where Senior Judge Lush stated at para 85 that "*In the context of testate succession, at least, the principle that deputies should interfere with succession rights as little as possible is compatible with the principle set out in section 1(5) of the Act, namely, that an act done or decision made for or on behalf of a person who lacks capacity must be done or made in their best interests*".

The Law Society has produced a helpful Practice Note entitled "Access and Disclosure of an Incapacitated Person's Will" which is available online.[44] The Practice Note provides guidance to clarify when a solicitor can disclose a copy of a client's will to a property and affairs attorney or deputy where the client has lost capacity. In summary, a solicitor should generally disclose the client's will to such an attorney or deputy because they are acting as agent for the client, but exceptionally they should not do so (unless ordered to do so by the Court of Protection) where:

(1) The client, when they retained capacity, made it clear that their will is not to be disclosed prior to their death.

(2) The LPA or EPA contains a restriction which prevents the attorney from acting until P lacks capacity to manage her property and financial affairs and there is not sufficient evidence to prove that restriction is satisfied.

(3) The solicitor is concerned that the attorney or deputy has acted, is acting or proposes to act in breach of their duties as set out in Chapter 7 of the Code of Practice.

Example

Peter made a will in which he gave his entire estate to his son Paul, excluding his daughter Pauline. Peter was subsequently involved in a car crash and sustains a brain injury which means that he now lacks testamentary capacity. Pauline was appointed to act as his deputy to manage his property and affairs. Pauline asks Peter's solicitor for a copy of Peter's will. Paul tells the solicitor that if Pauline discovers that she has been left out of the will then he is concerned that she might transfer some of Peter's assets to herself, in breach of her duties as deputy. The solicitor decides to apply to the Court of Protection for guidance as to whether he should disclose the will to Pauline.

[44] https://www.lawsociety.org.uk/en/topics/private-client/access-and-disclosure-of-an-incapacitated-persons-will

If no attorney or deputy is managing P's property and affairs, then P's will should not be disclosed to anyone unless authorised by the Court of Protection. Any application for authority for P's will to be disclosed should be made on Form COP1 (or Form COP9 if the application is made within existing proceedings), and the Court of Protection will only authorise disclosure if it is in P's best interests to do so.[45]

If P does not have a will, then on death her estate will be distributed under the rules of intestacy set out in section 46 of the Administration of Estates Act 1925. Those rules were substantially amended as regards anyone who dies on or after 1 October 2014 by virtue of the Inheritance and Trustees' Powers Act 2014. The government has a helpful website which identifies who is entitled to inherit under the rules of intestacy in any given case.[46] The rules of intestacy are simply a default set of rules which apply in the absence of a will, and it may well be in P's best interests to apply for a statutory will rather than to allow those default rules to apply.

[45] The best interests test is discussed in Chapter 3 of this book.

[46] https://www.gov.uk/inherits-someone-dies-without-will

CHAPTER THREE

WOULD IT BE IN P'S BEST INTERESTS FOR A STATUTORY WILL TO BE AUTHORISED AND, IF SO, ON WHAT TERMS?

In deciding whether to exercise its power to authorise a statutory will and, if so, in deciding what the terms of the statutory will should be, the Court of Protection must act in P's best interests. The concept of P's best interests was introduced by the MCA 2005 and is of critical importance in any application for a statutory will. The test is *not* what would be objectively reasonable for P to do, or what P might be expected to have done if he had capacity. It is what it is in P's best interests to do. The purpose of the best interests test is to consider matters from P's point of view.[47]

The concept of best interests is not defined in the MCA 2005, which reflects the fact that every person who lacks capacity, and every case, is different and must be decided on its own facts.[48] What the Act does say that P's best interests must *not* be determined merely on the basis of P's age or appearance, or a condition of his, or an aspect of his behaviour, which might lead others to make unjustified assumptions about what might be in his best interests.[49]

Instead of defining best interests, section 4 of the MCA 2005 sets out various steps which must be taken by the Court of Protection when determining whether it is P's best interests to authorise a statutory will

[47] See *Aintree University Hospitals NHS Foundation Trust v. James* [2013] UKSC 27; [2014] 1 AC 591 at para 45.

[48] See *Aintree University Hospitals NHS Foundation Trust v. James* [2013] UKSC 27; [2014] 1 AC 591 at para 36.

[49] See s.4(1) MCA 2005.

and, if so, on what terms. Having taken those steps, the Court of Protection "*must then form a value judgment of its own, giving effect to the paramount statutory instructions that any decision must be made in P's best interests*".[50] That value judgment involves the weighing of the various factors against each other in the balance before deciding where the balance falls.[51] In carrying out that weighing process it is sometimes helpful to draw up a "balance sheet", that is, a table of factors for and against the making of a statutory will.[52]

This process was discussed in *In Re M (Statutory Will)*[53] where the Judge emphasised that there is no hierarchy as between the various factors set out in section 4. The weight to be given to each step will depend upon the particular circumstances of the case. In some cases one or more steps may be of "magnetic importance" in influencing or even determining the outcome of the application.[54]

The steps which must be taken under section 4 of the MCA 2005 are as follows.

Step 1 – Consider all the relevant circumstances

Section 4(2) of the MCA 2005 states that the person who is making the determination of what is in P's best interests must consider all the relevant circumstances. It might be thought that this is so general as to be unhelpful, but it does make it clear that the Court of Protection can take into account other factors beyond those specifically mentioned in section 4 of the MCA 2005.

---

50 See *In Re P (Statutory Will)* [2009] EWHC 163 (Ch); [2010] Ch 33 at para 39.

51 See Re Meek [2014] COPLR 535 at para 36.

52 In *Re JC* [2012] COPLR 540 at para 53 Senior Judge Lush doubted the effectiveness of the balance sheet approach in statutory wills cases, whereas in *Re Meek* [2014] EWCOP 1; [2014] COPLR 535 at para 36 HHJ Hodge QC stated that he had found the balance sheet particularly helpful.

53 *In re M (Statutory Will)* [2009] EWHC 2525 (Fam); [2011] 1 WLR 344, at para 32.

54 In *Re JC* [2012] COPLR 540 Senior Judge Lush stated that in statutory will applications there is usually at least one factor of magnetic importance.

Example

Isabelle is aged 73 and lacks testamentary capacity. Before she lost capacity, she told her sister during a conversation that she would like to make a new will leaving her estate to her grandchildren. That verbal statement will be a relevant factor for the Court of Protection to take into account in determining whether it is in Isabelle's best interests to authorise a statutory will and if so on what terms, despite the fact that section 4(6)(a) of the MCA 2005 refers only to "any relevant written statement made by [P] when he had capacity".[55]

"Relevant circumstances" are defined by section 4(11) of the MCA 2005 as being those circumstances of which the Court of Protection is aware and which it would be reasonable to regard as relevant. The first limb of this definition serves to emphasise the importance of the parties providing evidence to the Court of Protection on any circumstance which they consider relevant.

Step 2 – Consider whether it is likely that P will at some time have capacity to make a will and, if so, when that is likely to be

Section 4(3) of the MCA 2005 states that the person determining P's best interests must consider (a) whether it is likely that P will at some time have capacity in relation to the matter in question, and (b) if it appears likely that he will, when that is likely to be. If it seems that P's loss of testamentary capacity is only temporary then it may be appropriate simply to wait for them to recover rather than applying for a statutory will. The Code of Practice sets out a helpful list of factors which may indicate that P may regain or develop capacity in the future.[56]

Step 3 – Permit and encourage P to participate, or improve his ability to participate, as fully as possible in the decision whether to make a statutory will and if so on what terms

---

[55] This example is taken from *In re M (Statutory Will)* [2009] EWHC 2525 (Fam); [2011] 1 WLR 344, at para 36.

[56] Code of Practice, para 5.28.

The mere fact that P lacks capacity does not mean that he can be ignored by the person determining his best interests. On the contrary, section 4(4) of the MCA 2005 states that the person determining P's best interests must, so far as reasonably practicable, permit and encourage the person to participate, or to improve his ability to participate, as fully as possible in any act done for him or any decision affecting him. The extent to which P will be able to participate in the decision-making process will differ in each case, and there will be some cases where P's condition is such that he will be unable to participate in any way. Chapter 3 of the Code of Conduct contains a raft of practical suggestions about how P can be encouraged to play as big a role as possible in the decision-making process.

Step 4 – Consider, so far as is reasonably ascertainable –

(a) P's past and present wishes and feelings (and, in particular, any relevant written statement made by him when he had capacity),

(b) the beliefs and values that would be likely to influence his decision if he had capacity, and

(c) the other factors that he would be likely to consider if he were able to do so.

This step, which is contained in section 4(6) of the MCA 2005, is of central importance in many statutory will applications and needs unpacking because it incorporates a number of different factors.

First, the Court of Protection is required to consider (so far as is reasonably ascertainable) P's *present* wishes and feelings. At first blush, it may be thought surprising that the Court should take into account the wishes and feelings of a person who lacks testamentary capacity. However the MCA 2005 recognises that the fact that a person lacks capacity to make a will does not mean that he is incapable of expressing wishes or feelings, or that any wishes and feelings that he is able to express should be disregarded. On the contrary, P's wishes and feelings will always be a significant factor to which the Court should play close regard. It is P's own wishes and feelings which are relevant, rather than what a reasonable person in P's position would think.[57]

If P's wishes and feelings are reasonably ascertainable, then the difficult question is what weight should be given to them when determining P's bests interests. This question has been discussed in a series of the leading cases[58], culminating in the case of *Re M (Statutory Will)*[59] where the Judge held that the weight to be attached to P's wishes and feelings will always be case-specific and fact-specific. In other words, it will depend upon the individual circumstances of the particular case. In determining the weight and importance to be given to P's wishes and feelings in any given case the Court of Protection should take into account all the relevant circumstances of the case, which will include the following specific factors:

(a) The degree of P's incapacity, for the nearer the borderline the more weight must in principle be attributed to P's wishes and feelings.

(b) The strength and consistency of the views being expressed by P.

(c) The possible impact on P of knowledge that her wishes and feelings are not being given effect to.

(d) The extent to which P's wishes and feelings are, or are not, rational, sensible, responsible and pragmatically capable of sensible implementation in the particular circumstances.

(e) Crucially, the extent to which P's wishes and feelings, if given effect to, can properly be accommodated within the court's overall assessment of what is in his best interests.

---

[57] See *Aintree University Hospitals NHS Foundation Trust v. James* [2013] UKSC 67; [2014] 1 AC 591, at para 45.

[58] The series of leading cases are *Re S* [2010] 1 WLR 1082; *Re P* [2009] EWHC 163 (Ch); [2010] Ch 33; and *In re M (Statutory Will)* [2009] EWHC 2525 (Fam); [2011] 1 WLR 344.

[59] *In re M (Statutory Will)* [2009] EWHC 2525 (Fam); [2011] 1 WLR 344, in particular at para 35.

Second, the Court of Protection is required to consider (so far as is reasonably ascertainable) P's *past* wishes and feelings, including in particular any relevant written statement made by him when he had capacity. In statutory will cases, any wills or codicils previously made by P are clearly relevant written statements which the Court should consider carefully. If there is a series of previous wills which show a consistent pattern, then that is likely to be particularly relevant. Even if a document is not executed as a valid will, it may nevertheless be a relevant statement to take into account.[60] But the Court of Protection is unlikely to take into account any previous will or codicil where there is real doubt about its validity because of lack of testamentary capacity, want of knowledge and approval or undue influence.[61]

Third, the Court of Protection is required to consider (so far as is reasonably ascertainable) the beliefs and values which would be likely to influence P's decision if he had capacity. It will be up to the parties to provide evidence to the Court to show what beliefs and values P had before he lacked capacity. They may include, for example, social, cultural or religious beliefs or values, or a history of giving money to charity.

Fourth, the Court of Protection must consider (so far as is reasonably ascertainable) the other factors which P would be likely to consider if he were able to do so. One particular factor which is discussed in a number of the statutory will cases is whether P would want to be remembered as having done "the right thing" by their will.[62] The general consensus

---

60 See *NT v. FS* [2013] EWHC 684 (COP); [2013] COPLR 313, where it was held that a document which FS described as his will, despite the fact that it had not been witnessed and so was invalid, should be taken into account under section 4(6) of the MCA 2005 in determining FS's best wishes.

61 See *In re D (Statutory Will)* [2010] EWHC 2159 (Ch); [2012] Ch 57 at para 16 where it was held that "*the weight to be given to [a previous will] will depend upon the circumstances under which it was prepared*".

62 The cases in which this is discussed are *Re P* [2009] EWHC 163 (Ch); [2010] Ch 33 at para 44; *Re M* [2009] EWHC 2525 (Fam); [2011] 1 WLR 344 at para 38; *Re G(TJ)* [2010] EWHC 3005; [2010] COPLR Con Vol 403 at para 53; *In re D (Statutory Will)* [2010] EWHC 2159 (Ch); [2012] Ch 57 at para 16; *Re JC* [2012] COPLR 540 at para 54; *NT v. FS* [2013] EWHC 684 (COP) at para 8; *Re Meek*

appears to be that this is a factor which can legitimately be taken into account, provided that there is no evidence to suggest that P did not want to do the right thing[63], and provided also that it is clear what the "right thing" to do is. So for example if P has made a will in favour of a carer who subsequently subjects him to financial abuse, "the right thing" is likely to be the execution of a statutory will which excludes the carer from benefit.[64] On the other hand, if the statutory will application involves a contest between members of the same family, "the right thing" to do may be a matter of serious dispute and may be difficult if not impossible to ascertain.[65] In the unusual case of Re JC[66] it was held that the concept of "doing the right thing" was of no assistance given that:

> "*JC has an appalling track record. He has spent his entire lifetime doing precisely 'the wrong thing' in his relationships with others, and his malevolence is such that he would probably relish the prospect of thwarting his children's designs on his estate and would rejoice at being remembered by them with disaffection.*"[67]

Step 5 – Take into account, if it is practicable and appropriate to consult them, the views of –

(a) anyone named by P as someone entitled to be consulted on the matter in question or on matters of that kind,

(b) anyone engaged in caring for P or interested in his welfare,

(c) any donee of a lasting power of attorney granted by P, and

(d) any deputy appointed for P by the Court,

[2014] EWCOP 1 at para 34; and *In the matter of Peter Jones* [2014] EWCOP 59 at para 60.

[63] See *In the matter of Peter Jones* [2014] EWCOP 59, where DJ Eldergill commented at para 65 that "*The onset of mental incapacity is not an opportunity for moral correction*".

[64] Compare the facts of *Re M (Statutory Will)* [2011] 1 WLR 344.

[65] See *Re G(TJ)* [2010] EWHC 3005 (COP) at para 53.

[66] *Re JC* [2012] COPLR 540.

[67] See para 54 of the judgment.

as to what would be in P's best interests and, in particular, as to the matters mentioned in subsection 4(6) of the MCA 2005.

This step is contained in section 4(7) of the MCA 2005. It is designed to ensure that relevant people are consulted before any decision is taken on a statutory will application. The relevant people are those set out in paragraphs (a) to (d) above, and persons "interested in P's welfare" will normally include P's family members and friends.

The purpose of the consultation is to find out what the relevant people's views are on P's best interests and to obtain evidence as to the matters set out in section 4(6) of the MCA 2005, i.e. P's past and present wishes and feelings, the beliefs and values that would be likely to influence his decision if he had capacity, and any other factors that he would be likely to consider if he were able to do so.[68]

It is up to the parties involved in any statutory will application to provide evidence that they have consulted the relevant persons and what the views of those persons are.

There are some cases where it will not be practicable or appropriate to consult all the persons on the list, as section 4(7) itself recognises. This will be the case where consultation is likely to be unduly onerous, contentious, futile or serve no useful purpose.[69] In such a case, it is suggested that the parties should explain in their witness evidence why any person falling within any of the categories set out in section 4(7) has not been consulted.

---

[68] See *Aintree University Hospitals NHS Foundation Trust v. James* [2013] UKSC 27; [2014] 1 AC 591 at para 24 where Lady Hale stated that the Act "*provide[s] for consultation with carers and others interested in the patient's welfare as to what would be in his best interests and in particular what his own views would have been*".

[69] See *Re Allen*, unreported, 21 July 2009, a decision of the former Senior Judge of the Court of Protection.

CHAPTER FOUR

WHEN SHOULD AN APPLICATION FOR A STATUTORY WILL BE MADE?

In theory there is no limit to the circumstances in which a statutory will may be authorised by the Court of Protection. If it is in P's best interests for a statutory will be executed on his behalf, then the Court of Protection will authorise it. In practice, however, there are certain scenarios which crop up with sufficient frequency that they merit particular consideration. The purpose of this chapter is to set out those scenarios and to give some indication of the approach which the Court of Protection may take to them based on the reported authorities.

Scenario 1 – Intestacy

It is estimated that around 40% of adults do not have a will.[70] If P does not have a will, then when he dies his property will be distributed in accordance with the intestacy rules, as discussed in Chapter 2 of this book. It is conceivable that P may have made a deliberate decision not to make a will so that his estate will pass in accordance with the intestacy rules, but that is rare and the Court of Protection is likely to require compelling evidence before accepting that P had made such a decision. More often, P does not have a will simply because he never got round to making one, or because of a superstitious fear that making a will may "tempt fate", or because an earlier will has been revoked (for example, by P getting married), or because P executed a will which was invalid for some reason (for example, because it was not executed correctly).

---

[70] See https://www.lawcom.gov.uk/project/wills/

The intestacy rules have been rightly described as a "blunt instrument".[71] The beneficiaries under the intestacy rules will be P's next of kin, with priority being given to the deceased's spouse and children followed by other relatives in decreasing order of proximity. The amounts given to the beneficiaries under the intestacy rules are fixed, and may not be appropriate in any particular case. A striking feature of the intestacy rules is that they do not make any provision for cohabitants, that is, for anyone living with P as man and wife but who is not married to P. Likewise the operation of the intestacy rules is often not satisfactory where P has remarried and have children from their first marriage.

In 2011 the Law Commission recommended a major reform of the intestacy rules.[72] Some of those recommendations were implemented by the Inheritance and Trustees' Powers Act 2014. However, the Law Commission's recommendation that cohabitants should in certain circumstances have the same entitlement as a spouse or civil partner has not been implemented and there is no sign that it will be implemented in the foreseeable future.

The upshot of all of this is that where P does not have a will, it is often in his best interests to apply for a statutory will on terms which reflect his particular circumstances rather than relying upon the blunt instrument of the intestacy rules.

Scenario 2 – A significant change of circumstances[73]

People are often prompted into making a will by a significant life event, such as a marriage or civil partnership, a divorce or separation, the birth

---

[71] See para 1.11 of the Law Commission's Consultation Paper 231 entitled "Making a will" available online at https://www.lawcom.gov.uk/project/wills/

[72] For details see https://www.lawcom.gov.uk/project/intestacy-and-family-provision-claims-on-death/

[73] See *In Re D (Statutory Will)* [2010] EWHC 2159 (Ch); [2012] Ch 57 at para 7 where District Judge Ashton is recorded as having stated that it was "*only the role of the Court of Protection to authorise a statutory will when there has been a material change of circumstances which make existing testamentary provision inadequate or there is a vacuum*".

of children, or the death of family or friends, or by a significant change in their relationship with (or the financial circumstances of) potential beneficiaries. Where such a life event or change of relationship has occurred in P's life, it is often appropriate to undertake a review in order to determine whether it would be in P's best interests to apply for a statutory will. Thus in *Re HMF*[74], which is an old case decided before the MCA 2005 came into force, a statutory will application was prompted by the fact that P had made a will in favour of charities some 15 years earlier, but had since begun to take an interest in the surviving members of her family, namely two nephews, and had expressed a wish to make a will benefitting them.

Likewise a statutory will may be in P's best interests if there has been a significant change in the value of his estate, either upwards or downwards. A typical example of an upwards change in P's estate would be where P has received a substantial inheritance or gift, or an award of damages or compensation as a result of a court case. A typical example of a downwards change in P's estate is where P has moved into a residential care home and the fees have substantially reduced P's savings. In either case it would be prudent to review P's will (or the effect of the intestacy rules) and to consider whether it would be in P's best interests to apply for a statutory will.

Scenario 3 – Ademption

Ademption is the technical name for the failure of a specific gift contained in a will due to the fact that the subject matter of the gift no longer forms part of P's estate when he dies. So a specific gift of a property will in P's will would fail if P sells or gives away the property before he dies. Specific gifts of shares, money in a particular bank account, personal belongings or any other assets can likewise fail by ademption.

---

[74] *Re HMF* [1976] Ch 33; [1975] 2 all ER 795.

Example

Barbara makes a will leaving her house in London to her elder daughter, a very valuable painting to her younger daughter, and her residuary estate to her son. A few years later she sells the house in London and the painting, and uses the proceeds to buy a smaller bungalow to live in. When she dies, the gifts of the house in London and of the painting will both fail by ademption. As a result, any remaining proceeds of sale will form part of her residuary estate which will pass to her son.

In such circumstances it would often be in P's best interests to apply for a statutory will which will reflect the change in the nature of P's estate. A statutory will was authorised for precisely this reason in *Re D(J)*[75], a rather old case which was decided in 1981 before the MCA 2005 came into force. P in that case had made a will giving her house to a daughter who was caring for her. The house was subsequently sold, which resulted in the gift in favour of the daughter failing by ademption. The Court of Protection directed that a statutory will should be executed on terms which left a substantial legacy to the daughter in place of the gift of the house.

Paragraph 8 of Schedule 2 to the MCA 2005 contains a specific anti-ademption provision, the effect of which is to prevent ademption from occurring where the subject-matter of a gift contained in a will is disposed of during P's lifetime pursuant to section 18 of the MCA 2005.[76] This would include any disposal made by a deputy appointed to manage P's property and affairs, as well as disposals specifically authorised by the Court of Protection. The beneficiary of the gift in the will takes the same interest, if and so far as circumstances allow, in the property belonging to P's estate which represents the property disposed of. Paragraph 8(6) of

[75] [1982] Ch 237. Note that the case was decided using the old "substituted judgment" test which applied under the Mental Health Act 1983. That test has now been replaced by the "best interest" test under the MCA 2005.

[76] See the discussion of this provision in *Heywood & Massey: Court of Protection Practice* at 26-023.

Schedule 2 gives the Court of Protection power to give directions to facilitate this, such as money being paid into a separate account. However, the Court of Protection has indicated that, rather than giving such directions, it generally prefers to deal with the preservation of specific gifts as part of an application for a statutory will, because it enables the Court to consider the entire picture and gives the Court a wider discretion.[77]

Example

Barbara makes a will leaving her house in London to her elder daughter, a very valuable painting to her younger daughter, and her residuary estate to her son. Barbara subsequently loses capacity to manage her property and affairs and the Court of Protection appoints David to act as her deputy. David as deputy sells the house in London and the painting, and uses the proceeds to buy a smaller bungalow for Barbara to live in. When Barbara dies, the gift of the house in London and of the painting would not fail by ademption. Instead, such part of the bungalow as represents the proceeds of sale of the house in London, together with any remaining balance of the proceeds of sale of the house in London, would pass the elder daughter. Such part of the bungalow as represents the proceeds of the painting, together with any remaining balance of the proceeds of sale of painting, would pass the younger daughter. The remaining residuary estate would pass to the son. Compare this outcome to the previous example in the box above.

Importantly, the anti-ademption provision discussed above does *not* apply to a disposal by an attorney appointed to manage P's property and affairs under a Lasting Power of Attorney (or an Enduring Power of Attorney). This is illustrated by the case of *Banks v. NatWest Bank*.[78] In that case P had made a will giving her property to her daughter, and had also appointed the same daughter to act as her attorney under an

[77] See *Re D* [2004] WTLR 643. Note that this case was decided under the Mental Health Act 1983, but it is thought that the same approach would be taken under the MCA 2005.

[78] [2005] EWHC 3479 (Ch).

Enduring Power of Attorney. When P lost capacity to manage her affairs, the daughter, acting as attorney, sold the property, and used the proceeds of sale to purchase bonds. When P died, the daughter sought to argue that she was entitled to the bonds. That argument failed. The Court held that the sale of the property had adeemed the gift.

This is a cautionary tale for attorneys. If an attorney is considering a sale of P's asset, and suspects or knows that the sale will cause a specific gift in P's will to adeem, then the attorney should consider applying for an order authorising the sale under section 18 of the MCA 2005 (which would then bring the anti-ademption provision discussed above into play), together with any appropriate directions under paragraph 8(6) of Schedule 2 to the MCA 2005 (as discussed above), or alternatively, and perhaps preferably, should apply for a statutory will.

Scenario 4 – Doubts over the validity of P's existing will

It is now established that the Court of Protection can direct the execution of a statutory will in any case where there is dispute or uncertainty as to the validity of a recent will due to concerns about a possible lack of testamentary capacity, want of knowledge and approval, or the possible exercise of undue influence.

This principle was established in 2010 in the case of *In re D (Statutory Will)*[79]. In that case P was a lady who had made a valid will in 1995 dividing her estate between her 3 children. She made two further wills in 2004 and 2006, the first of which left her entire estate to her younger daughter and the second of which left her estate to the younger daughter and her son. There were real doubts about the validity of the 2004 and 2006 wills. The Court of Protection held that those doubts were sufficient to mean that it should set to rest all concerns about P's true testamentary wishes by ordering the execution of a statutory will on similar terms to her 1995 will. The Judge stated that it was in P's best wishes to take this course "*rather than leaving her estate to be eroded by the costs of litigation after her death, and her memory to be tainted by the*

[79] *In re D (Statutory Will)* [2010] EWHC 2159 (Ch); [2012] Ch 57.

bitterness of a contested probate dispute between her children (which may extend to members of the next generation)".[80]

In order to engage this principle, it is only necessary to establish that there are sufficient doubts about the earlier will (or wills) to mean that it would be in P's best interests to direct a statutory will. The Court of Protection has no power to rule on the validity of the previous will, and it is unlikely to embark upon a detailed investigation of all the evidence necessary to resolve a dispute as to the validity of the previous will. In other words, the Court of Protection will not allow the statutory will application to turn into a contentious probate trial.

There are however limits to this principle. The Judge stated in *In re D (Statutory Will)* itself that "*the existence and nature of the dispute, and the ability of the Court of Protection to investigate the issues which underlie it, are clearly relevant factors to be taken into account when deciding whether, overall, it is in the protected person's best interests to order the execution of a statutory will*".

Example

Terry is a farmer who many years ago made a will dividing his estate equally between his son and two daughters. More recently, at a time when Terry was exhibiting the early signs of dementia, he made a new will leaving his farm (which is by far his most valuable asset) to his son, and his residuary estate to his daughters. Terry now lacks testamentary capacity. When the daughters find out about the new will, they apply for a statutory will. The son says that even if the new will is invalid, he intends to bring a proprietary estoppel claim to the farm or a claim under the Inheritance (Provision for Family and Dependants) Act 1975 when Terry dies. In deciding whether to direct a statutory will, the Court of Protection will consider what doubts exist about the validity of the new will, and whether it is able to investigate the issues which underlie the son's intended claims.

[80] See para 21 of the judgment.

Scenario 5 – Financial abuse or other wrongdoing

It is a sad fact that those who lack capacity to manage their own property and affairs are sometimes subject to financial abuse or other wrongdoing. A striking example of such a case is *Re Meek.*[81] Mrs Meek suffered from vascular dementia and lived in a care home. MJ and JM, who were related to Mrs Meek by marriage, were appointed to act as her deputies. They took advantage of that position by making extensive gifts from Mrs Meek's estate to themselves and their family members, conduct which was described by the Judge as being "*tantamount to daylight robbery*".[82] When this misconduct was discovered, the Court of Protection removed MJ and JM as deputies and ordered them to repay some £204,000 to Mrs Meek.[83] The Judge at that hearing advised MJ and JM to apply for a statutory will, saying that a statutory will was "*the missing piece in the jigsaw and, until it is in place, the picture is incomplete*".[84] In fact it was Mrs Meek's new deputy who subsequently applied for a statutory will, and that application was granted. MJ and JM were excluded from benefit under that statutory will, with the Judge commenting that "*I have no doubt that Mrs Meek would have been appalled by their behaviour had she been able to know and appreciate its nature…*".[85]

Scenario 6 – Tax planning

It may be in P's best interests to direct a statutory will in terms which will reduce or extinguish the tax liability borne by P's estate on his death. Whether it will be in P's best interests to direct a statutory will for achieve such tax benefit will depend upon applying the best interests test in section 4 of the MCA in the circumstances of each case, including in particular whether P has previously engaged in tax planning or expressed any wish to do so. In the case of *Re JMA*[86], the Court of Protection

---

[81] *Re Meek* [2014] EWCOP 1; [2014] COPLR 535.

[82] See the judgment in *Re Meek* at para 72.

[83] *Re GM* [2013] COPLR 290.

[84] See the judgment in *Re GM* at paras 100 and 101.

[85] See the judgment in *Re Meek* at para 74.

[86] *Re JMA* [2018] EWCOP 19; [2018] COPLR 428.

rejected the argument that it should proceed on the basis of a general assumption that most people are motivated by a desire to save tax if that benefits their relatives. The Judge stated:

> "Mitigation of tax, particularly taxes of inter-generational effect and even by completely lawful 'vanilla' means, is a matter on which there may be a range of views. The Mental Capacity Act 2005 does not permit the court to rely on default positions, assumptions or generalisations in making a decision about whether gifts to effect tax mitigation are in the best interests of a particular protected person. The court must decide the application on nothing more and nothing less than a case-specific application of s 4."[87]

The reported cases on tax planning concern applications for authority to make gifts or to create trusts (otherwise known as settlements) during P's lifetime, rather than statutory wills.[88] That is not surprising because tax planning often involves transferring assets out of P's estate during P's lifetime so that those assets are not taxed as part of P's estate when P dies. In determining whether to authorise lifetime gifts the Court of Protection will be especially concerned to ensure that the gifs are affordable, in the sense that P will still retain sufficient assets comfortably to maintain himself even after the gifts have been made. That is self-evidently not a consideration in any statutory will application where the statutory will only takes effect on P's death.

---

[87] See the judgment in *Re JMA* at para 66.

[88] The reported cases are *Re G(TJ)* [2010] EWHC 3005 (COP); [2010] COPLR Con Vol 403 at para 62; *Re JDS* [2012] EWHC 302 (COP); [2012] COPLR 383 (where a proposed gift for tax planning purposes was refused where P's estate consisted of compensation for a personal injury sustained by P); and *Re JMA* [2018] EWCOP 19; [2018] COPLR 428 (where a proposed gift for tax planning purposes was authorised where P had a multi-million pound estate).

CHAPTER FIVE

DOES YOUR CASE INVOLVE AN INTERNATIONAL ELEMENT?

This Chapter addresses two separate questions. The first is the effect of a statutory will in so far as it relates to property situated outside of England and Wales or where P is domiciled outside of England and Wales. The second is whether a statutory will or an equivalent document authorised by a foreign court will be recognised and enforced in England and Wales.

Foreign property/domicile

According to the law of England and Wales, the effect of a statutory will which disposes of property abroad or where P is domiciled abroad is set out in sub-paragraphs 4(3), 4(4) and 4(5) of Schedule 2 to the MCA 2005, which provide as follows:

> "*(3) The will has the same effect for all purposes as if –*
>
> > *(a) P had had the capacity to make a valid will, and*
> >
> > *(b) The will had been executed by him in the manner required by the 1837 Act.*
>
> *(4) But sub-paragraph (3) does not have effect in relation to the will –*
>
> > *(a) in so far as it disposes of immovable property outside England and Wales, or*
> >
> > *(b) in so far as it relates to any other property or matter if, when the will is executed –*
> >
> > > *(i) P is domiciled outside England and Wales, and*
> > >
> > > *(ii) The condition in sub-paragraph (5) is met.*

> *(5) The condition is that, under the law of P's domicile, any question of his testamentary capacity would fall to be determined in accordance with the law of a place outside England and Wales."*

These provisions are based upon 2 key concepts taken from English private international law. The first is the classification of property as movable or immovable.[89] This distinction is based upon whether or not the property is physically capable of being moved. Thus a freehold house is immovable property, whereas money in a bank account will be movable property. That said, the laws of different countries may differ as to which side of the line any particular piece of property should fall. In the event of a dispute as to whether property is movable or immovable, the law of the country in which the property is situated will decide the question.

The second key concept is domicile. According to English law every person must at all times have a single domicile. A person is domiciled in whichever country he either has, or is deemed by law to have, his permanent home.[90] A person receives a domicile of origin at birth[91], but can subsequently acquire a domicile of choice by moving to another country and intending to remain there indefinitely.[92] Any dispute over where P is domiciled in any particular case will be determined by English law.[93]

In the case of *In Re P (Statutory Will)*[94] the court had to consider how paragraph 4(4) above applied to a statutory will executed on behalf of P who was domiciled in California but related to immovable property in England and Wales. This depended upon whether "any other property" in paragraph 4(4)(b) means property of any description (whether movable or immovable) or is restricted to movable property, on the basis

---

[89] See Halsbury's Laws, Vol.19 (2011), at paras 676 onwards; and Dicey, Morris & Collins on the Conflict of Laws (15th ed.) at Chapter 22.

[90] Halsbury's Laws, Vol 19 (2011), at para 336.

[91] Halsbury's Laws, Vol 19 (2011), at para 341.

[92] Halsbury's Laws, Vol 19 (2011), at para 342.

[93] Halsbury's Laws, Vol 19 (2011), at para 338.

[94] *In re P (Statutory Will)* [2009] EWHC 163 (Ch); [2010] Ch 33.

that immovable property has already been dealt with in paragraph 4(4)(a). It was held that the latter interpretation was correct. The Judge held that:

> "*Under the previous legislation (section 97(4) of the 1983 Act) it was clear that the court did have power to order the execution of a will dealing with immovable property situated within England and Wales irrespective of the patient's domicile. Nothing in the travaux preparatoires leading to the passing of the Act, including the debates in Parliament, suggest that Parliament had any intention to change the law in this respect. Moreover, there is a general principle that in case of ambiguity in an Act of Parliament, it is to be assumed that Parliament intended the most continuity with the pre-existing law...*"[95]

The upshot of this analysis is as follows.

As regards immovable property, a statutory will has effect in so far as it disposes of immovable property situated in England and Wales, but will not have effect in so far as it disposes of immovable property situated in any other country. This is irrespective of where P is domiciled.

As regards movable property, a statutory will has effect if P is domiciled in England and Wales. If P is domiciled in any other country, then a statutory will has effect only if the law of P's domicile provides that the issue of his testamentary capacity should be determined by the law of England and Wales.

This can be illustrated by the following examples.

---

95 Para 34 of the judgment.

Example 1

Brigitte is a lady domiciled in France who lacks testamentary capacity by reason of dementia. She lives in a flat in Paris. She also owns a leasehold flat in London and holds a bank account with a bank in London. If the Court of Protection authorises a statutory will to be executed on Brigitte's behalf, then its effect will be as follows:

(1) The statutory will would have no effect in relation to Brigitte's flat in Paris, since the flat is immovable property situated outside of England and Wales.

(2) The statutory will would have effect in relation to Brigitte's leasehold flat in London, because it is immovable property situated in England and Wales.

(3) The bank account in London is movable property. Since Brigitte is domiciled in France, the statutory will would only have effect in relation to the bank account if the law of France provides that the issue of Brigitte's testamentary capacity should be determined by the law of England and Wales. Advice would need to be taken from a French lawyer to determine whether this condition is satisfied.

(4) The appointment of any executors in the statutory will would similarly only have effect if the law of France provides that the issue of P's testamentary capacity should be determined by the law of England and Wales. This is because the appointment of executors falls within "any other matter" as referred to in paragraph 4(4)(b) above.

Example 2

Jim lives in Bristol and is domiciled in England. He lacks testamentary capacity by reason of injuries sustained in a car accident. He owns a holiday house in Spain which contains a number of valuable paintings. If the Court of Protection authorises a statutory will to be executed on Jim's behalf then its effect would be as follows:

(1) The statutory will would have no effect in relation to Jim's holiday house in Spain, because it is immovable property situated outside of England and Wales.

(2) The statutory will would have effect in relation to the valuable paintings, because they are movable property and Jim is domiciled in England.

The rules set out above are the law of England and Wales. Whether a foreign court would regard a statutory will made in this country as valid and effective is a matter of the law in that country. Advice should be sought from an appropriately qualified lawyer in that country.

Recognition of foreign statutory wills or equivalent

In practice this issue does not arise frequently, not least because the concept of a statutory will is unknown in many jurisdictions. Schedule 3 to the MCA 2005 provides for the court in England and Wales to recognise and enforce "protective measures" taken in another country provided that the adult in question is habitually resident in that jurisdiction. However it remains unclear whether a statutory will would qualify as a "protective measure" for these purposes, and there appears to be no authority on this issue.[96]

If Schedule 3 to the MCA 2005 does not apply then the general principles of English private international law would apply. Those principles distinguish between the capacity to make a will (which would

[96] See the (inconclusive) discussion in Heywood & Massey's Court of Protection Practice at paras 14.016 onwards.

include a court's power to authorise a third party to execute a will on P's behalf) and formal validity of the will (such as whether it has been signed and witnessed). P's capacity to make a will in relation to movables is governed by the law of P's domicile at the time of execution of the will.[97] P's capacity to make a will in relation to immovables is probably governed by the law of the country in which the immovables are situated, although there is no authority on point.[98] The formal validity of the will is governed by P's domicile at the date of death.[99]

[97] See Rule 151 in Dicey, Morris & Collins on the Conflict of Laws (15th ed.).

[98] See Dicey, Morris & Collins, above, at 27-025.

[99] See Rule 152 in Dicey, Morris & Collins, above.

CHAPTER SIX

WHAT PROCEDURE SHOULD BE FOLLOWED WHEN APPLYING FOR A STATUTORY WILL?

This Chapter sets out the procedure that should be followed by any applicant applying for a statutory will, and by any other parties involved in such an application. The procedure is governed by the MCA 2005, the Court of Protection Rules 2017 and Practice Directions, including in particular Practice Direction 9E which concerns applications relating to statutory will and codicils. All these materials are freely available online.[100] The procedure also involves a number of standard forms (known as Form COP1, Form COP3, etc.) which again are freely available online.[101] Most of the forms are accompanied by Guidance Notes which should be read carefully before the form is completed.

There are two fundamental principles which underpin the procedure in the Court of Protection. The first is the overriding objective of enabling the court to deal with a case justly and at proportionate cost, having regard to the principles contained in the MCA 2005.[102] The second is the need for the court to consider what directions it should make in order to encourage P's participation in the court process, notwithstanding that P may lack capacity to litigate or to take the decision in question.

---

[100] The MCA 2005 is available at https://www.legislation.gov.uk/ukpga/2005/9/contents The Court of Protection Rules 2017 are available at https://www.legislation.gov.uk/uksi/2017/1035/contents/made The Practice Directions, including Practice Direction 9E, are available at https://www.judiciary.uk/publications/court-of-protection-practice-directions/

[101] The forms are available at https://www.gov.uk/government/collections/court-of-protection-forms

[102] Rule 1.1 of the Court of Protection Rules 2017.

The procedure for applying for a statutory will is set out below in a series of steps, which it is suggested anyone involved in such an application should work through methodically. It is assumed that P is an adult who lacks testamentary capacity, those being two basic requirements which must be satisfied before the Court of Protection will have power to authorise a statutory will, as discussed in Chapter 1 of this book.

STEP 1 – Who can bring the application and do they need permission?

There is no limit on who can apply for a statutory will, although in practice such applications are usually made by P's deputy, P's attorney under a Lasting Power of Attorney or Enduring Power of Attorney, or one of P's family members or friends who is either a beneficiary under an existing will or a proposed beneficiary under the statutory will.

Permission is not required to make the application. Rule 8.2(b)(i) of the Court of Protection Rules 2017 expressly states that permission is not required for any application concerning P's property and affairs, which would include an application for a statutory will.[103]

STEP 2 – What steps should be followed before the application is issued?

There is no set procedure or protocol which must be followed before a statutory will application is issued. Practice Direction 3B sets out three Case Pathways, two of which include a pre-issue stage which requires an applicant to carry out certain specified steps, but applications for statutory wills are expressly excluded from Practice Direction 3B.[104]

That said, if time permits, it is both courteous and prudent for anyone who intends to issue a statutory will application to write to the proposed

---

[103] Rule 8.2 of the Court of Protection Rules 2017 and s.50 of the MCA 2005 state that certain specified persons do not need to apply for permission to make an application to the Court of Protection, but those provisions lose their significance in statutory will applications in light of the rule that permission is not required if the application concerns P's property and affairs.

[104] See para 1.1 of Practice Direction 3B.

respondents[105] to the application in order to notify them of the proposed application and to canvass their views. Their views are likely to be taken into account by the Court of Protection under section 4(7) of the MCA 2005 in determining whether it would be in P's best interests to authorise a statutory will and if so in what terms, and so it is preferable for the applicant to know what those views are before deciding whether to launch an application. Pre-action correspondence often narrows the issues in dispute and, in some cases, it may be possible to agree on the terms of a statutory will before the proceedings are issued, perhaps by using the Court of Protection Mediation Pilot Scheme[106], as discussed in Chapter 10 of this book. Any agreed statutory will would require the approval of the Court of Protection in order to be effective.

STEP 3 – Issuing the application

The applicant makes the application by filing the application form and the other documents set out below, and paying the application fee which currently stands at £365.[107]

The application form and other documents which the Applicant has to file are as follows:

(1) the application form (Form COP1).

(2) Annex A (Form COP1A);

(3) Annex C (Form COP1C);

(4) The capacity assessment (Form COP3).

(5) Witness statement (Form COP24).

[105] The identification of respondents is discussed in Step 3 below.

[106] Details of which are available online at https://www.courtofprotectionmediation.uk

[107] The application fee is prescribed by the Court of Protection Fees Order 2007, Article 4 and Schedule 1. Helpful guidance on fees is contained in Form COP44 "Court of Protection fees" which is available online at https://www.gov.uk/government/publications/court-of-protection-fees-cop44

These are discussed in turn below.

The documents should be filed at the Court of Protection's central registry at First Avenue House, either by post or at the public counter. The contact details are as follows:

Address:
PO Box 70185
First Avenue House
42-49 High Holborn
London
WC1A 9JA

Enquiries:
courtofprotectionenquiries@justice.gov.uk

Telephone:
0300 456 4600

Website:
https://www.find-court-tribunal.service.gov.uk/courts/court-of-protection

(1) The application form (Form COP1)

The application is made on Form COP1.[108]

Form COP1 is divided into 8 sections, each of which asks various questions which the applicant should answer in the boxes next to the questions. There are guidance notes at the end of the form which the applicant should read carefully before completing the form.

The applicant must sign the statement of truth which is included at the end of Form COP1 in the following form:[109]

---

[108] If the application is made within existing proceedings, then Form COP9 should be used instead.

[109] Rule 5.2 and 5.4 of the Court of Protection Rules 2017.

> *"[I believe] [The applicant(s) believe(s)] that the facts stated in this application form and its annex(es) are true."*

Proceedings for contempt of court may be brought against a person if that person makes, or causes to be made, a false statement in a witness statement verified by a statement of truth without an honest belief in its truth.[110]

In practice the only part of Form COP1 which gives rise to any difficulty is Section 5, which asks for details of the respondents who are to be served with the application and the persons who are to be notified of the application. The question is: who should the applicant name as respondents and persons to be notified?

The distinction between a respondent and a person to be notified is that a respondent will automatically become a party to the proceedings if he or she acknowledges service, whereas a person to be notified will not be a party to the proceedings unless he or she applies to be joined as a party. The two categories are mutually exclusive, so a person named as respondent should not also be named as a person to be notified.[111]

Respondents

The general rule set out in rule 9.3(c)(iii) of the Court of Protection Rules 2017 is that the application form should name as a respondent any person (other than P) whom the applicant reasonably believes to have an interest which means that that person ought to be heard in relation to the application.

This is expanded upon in relation to statutory wills applications by paragraph 9 of Practice Direction 9E, which states that the applicant must name as respondent:

---

[110] Rule 5.6 of the Court of Protection Rules 2017.

[111] See Practice Direction 9B, para 3.

(a) any beneficiary under an existing will or codicil who is likely to be materially or adversely affected by the application;

(b) any beneficiary under a proposed will or codicil who is likely to be materially or adversely affected by the application; and

(c) any prospective beneficiary under P's intestacy where P has no existing will.

Unless the court orders otherwise, P should not be named as a respondent.[112]

Persons to be notified

Practice Direction 9B explains who should be named as persons to be notified. It states that the applicant should identify at least 3 persons who are likely to have an interest in being notified that an application form has been issued.[113] It should be presumed that members of P's close family will be interested in being notified unless the applicant is aware of circumstances which suggest otherwise, such as where the applicant is aware that the relative in question has had little or no involvement in P's life and has shown no inclination to do so.[114]

Paragraph 7 of Practice Direction 9B sets out the following list of people ordered according to their presumed closeness in terms of relationship to P. They should be notified in descending order (as appropriate to P's circumstances):

(a) spouse or civil partner;

(b) person who is not a spouse or a civil partner but who has been living with P as if they were;

(c) parent or guardian;

---

[112] Rule 9.13(4) of the Court of Protection Rules 2017.

[113] Practice Direction 9B, para 4.

[114] Practice Direction 9B, para 5.

(d) child;

(e) brother or sister;

(f) grandparent or grandchild;

(g) aunt or uncle;

(h) child of a person falling within sub-paragraph (e);

(i) step-parent; and

(j) half-brother or half-sister.

Where the applicant decides that a person listed in one of the above categories should be notified, then all other persons in that same category should also be notified unless there is a good reason not to do so.[115]

In addition to the list above, the following persons must be notified where appropriate:[116]

(a) Where P is under 18, any person with parental responsibility for P within the meaning of the Children Act 1989.[117]

(b) Any legal or natural person who is likely to be affected by the outcome of any application.

(c) Any deputy appointed by the court, an attorney appointed under an enduring power of attorney or a donee of a lasting power of attorney (where that person has power to make decisions on behalf of P in regard to a matter to which the application relates).

(d) Any other person not already mentioned whom the applicant reasonably considers has an interest in being notified that an application form has been issued.

---

[115] Practice Direction 9B, para 8.

[116] Practice Direction 9B, para 10.

[117] This will not apply in a statutory will application since the Court cannot authorise a statutory will for P unless he or she is aged 18 or over, as discussed in Chapter 1 of this book.

Where the applicant choses not to notify a person listed in either of the 2 lists above, the evidence in the application form must set out why that person was not notified.[118]

Example

Fred is an 80 year old farmer who lacks testamentary capacity by reason of Alzheimer's Disease. He has a previous will in which he gave a substantial legacy to the RSPCA and left his residuary estate to his wife for her life, and upon her death to be divided between his 3 sons. His wife died long ago and he subsequently formed a relationship with Rachel with whom he has been living as man and wife. Fred is estranged from one of his sons, but is close to his other 2 sons. Fred's parents are dead but he has a sister and brother who are both alive, although his brother lives in Australia and Fred has had no contact with him for many years. Rachel applies for a statutory will leaving legacies to both the RSPCA and the Alzheimer's Society, and dividing the residuary estate as to 50% to herself and as to 50% to the 2 sons with whom Fred remains on good terms.

Rachel names as respondents the RSPCA, the Alzheimer's Society and Fred's 3 sons.

Rachel names as persons to be notified Fred's sister, and Fred's sister's 2 adult children.

Rachel explains in her witness statement that she has not named Fred's brother or Fred's brother's children as persons to be notified because they live in Australia and Fred has had no contact with them for many years.

(2) Annex A (Form COP1A)

Form COP1A is a standard form for all property and affairs applications which asks for details of P's financial circumstances. It must be completed

[118] Practice Direction 9B, paras 9 and 11.

and filed with any application for an order relating to P's property and affairs, which includes statutory will applications.[119]

(3) Annex C (Form COP1C)

Form COP1C sets out details of the information which the applicant must provide to support the application[120], as follows:

(a) a medical report on the current testamentary capacity of the person to whom the application relates;

(b) COP24 witness statement setting out evidence in support of the application and confirmation that the person to whom the application relates is domiciled in England and Wales;[121]

(c) COP1A or a summary schedule of assets and their value, annual income and expenditure of the person to whom the application relates;

(d) Copy of all previous and existing wills and codicils;

(e) Draft proposed statutory will or codicil;

(f) Consent to act by proposed executor(s);

(g) Details of P's family with full names and dates of birth, where known (preferably in the form of a family tree.

There is an overlap between this information and the information which is required to be included in (or attached as exhibits to) the COP24 witness statement. There is no need to produce the information and documents twice: it will suffice if it is either annexed to the Form

[119] See the table in Practice Direction 9A, para 12.

[120] The requirement to file Annex C with the application is contained in the table in Practice Direction 9A, para 12.

[121] Although there are situations in which the Court of Protection can authorise an effective statutory will where P is domiciled abroad, as discussed in Chapter 5.

COP1C or included in (or attached as exhibits to) the COP24 witness statement.[122]

Drafting the proposed statutory will

As stated above, the information required by Form COP1C includes a draft of the proposed statutory will or codicil. The Annex to Practice Direction 9E contains a useful form of a statutory will which should be amended as appropriate to the particular case. The form only shows the manner in which the authorised person makes the will and executes the same. It is up to the applicant to draft the main provisions of the will, and it is suggested that the applicant should consult the standard will writing textbooks in order to do this.[123] The form is reproduced here for easc of reference:

> This is the last will of me AB [the person who lacks capacity] of …………. acting by CD the person authorised in that behalf by an order dated the …….. day of …………………… 20…….. made under the Mental Capacity Act 2005.
>
> I revoke all my former wills and codicils and declare this to be my last will.
>
> 1. I appoint EF and GH to be executors and trustees of this my will.
>
> 2. I give ……………
>
> In witness of which this will is signed by me AB acting by CD under the order mentioned above on [date].
>
> Signed by the said AB [the person who lacks capacity] by the said CD [authorised person] and by the said CD with [his/her] own name pursuant to the said order in our presence and attested by us in the presence of the said CD

---

[122] See Practice Direction 9E, para 8.

[123] See, for example, Williams on Wills (10th ed.) Vol.2, The Encyclopaedia of Forms and Precedents Vol.42(1), Parker's Will Precedents (10th ed.), and Drafting Trusts and Will Trusts: A Modern Approach (14th ed.).

[signature of AB]

[signature of CD]

[names and addresses of witness]

Sealed with the official seal of the Court of Protection the .... day of .... 20.........

(4) The capacity assessment (Form COP3)

This is the form which confirms that P lacks testamentary capacity. The reader is referred to Chapter 1 of this book which contains a discussion of the test for testamentary capacity and how the assessment should be carried out.

(5) Witness statement (Form COP24)

Form COP24 is the standard form used for witness statements in the Court of Protection. It contains a large box which is designed to contain the witness's evidence, although in practice witnesses commonly prepare witness statements in Word format which are then attached to Form COP24.

Practice Direction 9E states that the witness statement should include the following information, attaching documents as exhibits where necessary:[124]

(a) a copy of the draft will or codicil, plus one copy;[125]

---

124 Practice Direction 9E, para 6.

125 See the next section for an example form of a statutory will.

(b) a copy of any existing will or codicil;

(c) any consents to act by proposed executors;

(d) details of P's family, preferably in the form of a family tree, including details of the full name and date of birth of each person included in the family tree;

(e) a schedule showing details of P's current assets, with up to date valuations;

(f) a schedule showing the estimated net yearly income and spending of P;

(g) a statement showing P's needs, both current and future estimates, and P's general circumstances;

(h) if P is living in National Health Service accommodation, information on whether P may be discharged to local authority accommodation, to other fee-paying accommodation or to P's own home;

(i) if the applicant considers it relevant, full details of the resources of any proposed beneficiary, and details of any likely changes if the application is successful;

(j) details of any capital gains tax, inheritance tax or income tax which may be chargeable in respect of the subject matter of the application;

(k) ...[126]

(l) if appropriate, a statement of whether any land would be affected by the proposed will or settlement and if so, details of its location and title number, if applicable;

---

[126] Practice Direction 9E, para 6(k) refers to "an explanation of the effect, if any, that the proposed changes will have on P's circumstances, preferably in the form of a 'before and after' schedule of assets and income". This will not be relevant in relation to a statutory will application because the statutory will only takes effect on P's death.

(m)...[127]

(n) a copy of any registered enduring power of attorney or lasting power of attorney;

(o) confirmation that P is a resident of England or Wales;[128]

(p) an up to date report of P's present medical condition, life expectancy, likelihood of requiring increased expenditure in the foreseeable future, and testamentary capacity.

In addition to the specified information above, it is suggested that the witness statement should explain why the applicant considers that the proposed statutory will is in P's best interests. This should be done by reference to the best interests test in section 4 of the MCA 2005, as discussed in Chapter 3 and 4 of this book. To the extent that the witness statement seeks to record P's present wishes and feelings, the guidance set out in *ADS v. DSM*[129] discussed below under Step 7 below should be borne in mind.

The witness statement must be verified with a statement of truth, which is included as part of Form COP24, in the following form:[130]

> "*I believe that the facts stated in this witness statement are true.*"

Proceedings for contempt of court may be brought against a person if that person makes, or causes to be made, a false statement in a witness statement verified by a statement of truth without an honest belief in its truth.[131]

---

[127] Practice Direction 9E, para 7(m) only applies where the application is for a settlement of property or the variation of an existing settlement or trust. It therefore does not apply to an application for a statutory will.

[128] Although there are situations in which the Court of Protection can authorise an effective statutory will where P is domiciled abroad, as discussed in Chapter 5.

[129] *ADS v. DSM* [2017] EWCOP 8.

[130] Rules 5.2 and 5.5 of the Court of Protection Rules 2017.

[131] Rule 5.6 of the Court of Protection Rules 2017.

STEP 4 – Notifying P

Although P should not be named as a respondent to the application, the applicant[132] (or their duly appointed agent or such other person as the court may direct[133]) must notify P that an application form has been issued by the court.[134] Notification should be effected as soon as practicable and in any event within 14 days of the date on which the application form was issued.[135]

The person effecting notification must provide P personally[136] with the following information in a way that is appropriate to P's circumstances (for example, using simple language, visual aids or any other appropriate means):[137]

(1) P must be notified that an application form has been issued by the court.[138]

(2) The following matters should be explained to P:[139]

(a) who the applicant is;

(b) that the application raises the question of whether P lacks capacity in relation to a matter or matters, and what that means;

(c) what will happen if the court make the order or direction that has been applied for.

---

[132] Rule 7.2(1)(a) of the Court of Protection Rules 2017.

[133] Rule 7.2(1) of the Court of Protection Rules 2017.

[134] Rule 7.4(1) of the Court of Protection Rules 2017.

[135] Rule 7.8(3)(a) of the Court of Protection Rules 2017.

[136] Rule 7.8(2) of the Court of Protection Rules 2017.

[137] Rule 7.8(1) of the Court of Protection Rules 2017.

[138] Rule 7.4(1)(a) of the Court of Protection Rules 2017.

[139] Rule 7.4(2) of the Court of Protection Rules 2017.

(3) P must be informed that P may seek advice and assistance.[140]

P must be provided with a Form COP14 (which explains the matter for which notification is being provided) and a COP5 (to enable P to acknowledge notification).[141]

The applicant must thereafter file a certificate of service on Form COP20A[142] within 7 days beginning with the date on which the documents were served.[143]

The Court of Protection has the power to dispense with the requirement to notify P.[144] It may do so where, for example, P is in a permanent vegetative state or a minimally conscious state, or where notification by the applicant is likely to cause significant and disproportionate distress to P.[145]

STEP 5 – Serving Respondents

As soon as practicable and in any event within 14 days of the date on which the application form was issued, the applicant must serve anyone named in the application form as a respondent with a copy of the application form (Form COP1), copies of any other documents that have been filed with the court, and a Form COP5 for acknowledging service.[146]

The methods of service are set out in rule 6.3 of the Court of Protection Rules 2017. If it is not known whether a solicitor is acting on behalf of the respondent, then the documents may be served on the Respondent by delivering it personally, or by delivering it to their home address or

140 Rule 7.4(4) of the Court of Protection Rules 2017.

141 Rule 7.9 of the Court of Protection Rules 2017 and Practice Direction 7A, para 6.

142 Practice Direction 7A, para 7.

143 Rule 7.10(1) of the Court of Protection Rules 2017.

144 Rule 7.11 of the Court of Protection Rules 2017.

145 Practice Direction 7A, para 9.

146 Rule 9.6(1) of the Court of Protection Rules 2017.

last known home address, or by sending it to that address or last known address by first class post. Where a solicitor is authorised to accept service on behalf of a respondent, then the documents may be sent to the solicitor. The Court of Protection can direct service by an alternative method, including by document exchange or by electronic communication (such as email).[147] There are special rules regarding service out of the jurisdiction.[148]

The applicant must thereafter file a certificate of service on Form COP20B[149] within 7 days beginning with the date on which the documents were served.[150]

The court has power to dispense with service of the application.[151] Applications for the court to exercise this power are not uncommon, and are typically made where the individual who would ordinarily have to be served is a family member who no longer has contact with P or those caring for P, or has a poor relationship with them. The court considered such applications in two reported cases, namely *Re AB (Notification of Statutory Will Application)*[152] and *Re D*[153]. In both cases the application was refused, and the court emphasised that such applications would only be permitted in exceptional circumstances. If the applicant is afraid of the consequences to P or themselves then the court can exercise its powers to redact relevant details such as addresses.[154] If there are practical difficulties with service then consideration should be given to effecting service by means of an alternative method.[155]

---

147 Rule 6.3(4)-(6) of the Court of Protection Rules 2017 and Practice Direction 6A.

148 See rules 6.11 to 6.19 of the Court of Protection Rules 2017 and Practice Direction 6B.

149 Practice Direction 6A, para 16.

150 Rule 9.6(2) of the Court of Protection Rules 2017.

151 Rule 6.10 of the Court of Protection Rules 2017.

152 [2013] EWCOP B39.

153 [2016] EWCOP 35.

154 See rules 5.7 and 5.11 of the Court of Protection Rules 2017.

155 Rule 6.3(4)-(6) of the Court of Protection Rules 2017 and Practice Direction 6A.

STEP 6 – Notifying specified persons

As soon as reasonably practicable and in any event within 14 days of the date on which the application form was issued, the applicant must notify those persons specified in the application form as persons to be notified that an application has been issued, that it relates to the exercise of the court's jurisdiction in relation to P's property and affairs, and of the order(s) sought.[156]

Notification should be effected by sending each of the specified persons a completed Form COP15[157], accompanied by a form for acknowledging notification (Form COP5).[158]

The rules which apply to service on respondents (as discussed above) apply equally to notification of the specified persons.[159]

The applicant must thereafter file a certificate of service on Form COP20B[160] within 7 days beginning with the date on which the documents were served.[161]

STEP 7 – Responding to an application

Any person served with or notified of an application form and who wishes to take part in proceedings must file an Acknowledgment of Service/Notification (Form COP5).[162] This must be done not more than 14 days after the application form was served or notification of the application was given.[163] The court will then serve a copy of the Form

156 Rule 9.10(1) of the Court of Protection Rules 2017.

157 Practice Direction 9B, para 12.

158 Rule 9.10(2) of the Court of Protection Rules 2017.

159 Practice Direction 9B, para 13.

160 Practice Direction 6A, para 16.

161 Rule 9.10(3) of the Court of Protection Rules 2017.

162 Rule 9.12(1) of the Court of Protection Rules 2017.

163 Rule 9.12(2) of the Court of Protection Rules 2017.

COP5 on the applicant and any other persons who have served a Form COP5.[164]

If the person indicates in their Form COP5 that they oppose the application, then that person must file a witness statement containing any evidence upon which that person intends to rely.[165] Such a witness statement must be filed within 28 days of the application form being served or notification of the application being given. The witness statement should be on Form COP24, although it is common for a separate witness statement to be completed in Word format and attached to the Form COP24. Whilst there is no prescribed information which such a witness statement should contain, it should respond to the application by reference to P's best interests as set out in section 4 of the MCA 2005. To the extent that the witness statement seeks to record P's present wishes and feelings, the guidance set out in *ADS v. DSM*[166] discussed below under Step 7 should be borne in mind.

The witness statement must be verified with a statement of truth, which is included as part of Form COP24, in the following form:[167]

> "*I believe that the facts stated in this witness statement are true.*"

Proceedings for contempt of court may be brought against a person if that person makes, or causes to be made, a false statement in a witness statement verified by a statement of truth without an honest belief in its truth.[168]

---

[164] Rule 9.12(3) of the Court of Protection Rules 2017.

[165] Rule 19.12(5) of the Court of Protection Rules 2017.

[166] *ADS v. DSM* [2017] EWCOP 8.

[167] Rules 5.2 and 5.5 of the Court of Protection Rules 2017.

[168] Rule 5.6 of the Court of Protection Rules 2017.

STEP 8 – Joining P as a party and the involvement of the Official Solicitor

Paragraph 10 of Practice Direction E states that the court will consider at the earliest opportunity whether P should be joined as a party to the proceedings and, if P is so joined, the court will consider whether the Official Solicitor should be invited to act as a litigation friend, or whether some other person should be appointed as litigation friend.

A litigation friend is a person who is appointed by the court to make decisions on behalf of P about the court proceedings. Commonly the Official Solicitor is appointed to act as P's litigation friend. The Official Solicitor is a statutory office holder whose duties include acting as litigation friend for adults who lack capacity.

In most applications for statutory wills the court will invite the Official Solicitor to act as P's litigation friend, and the Official Solicitor usually accepts that invitation. The court will then usually direct that the applicant should serve a copy of the application and the other documents filed at court on the Official Solicitor. The Official Solicitor will then write to the applicant's solicitor requesting any further information she requires, and will make any further inquiries as she sees fit. She will usually also contact P (or the establishment where P resides) to obtain further information about P's circumstances and to ascertain any wishes and feelings that P is able to express which would be taken into account in determining P's best interests under section 4(6)(a) of the MCA 2005.

In *ADS v. DSM*[169], a statutory will case involving wide-ranging disputes of fact, the Court of Protection emphasised the need to ensure that anyone recording P's wishes and feelings should distinguish between matters of fact and assertion, and should try to ensure that P was not being influenced by members of her family. In particular, such a person should consider and take steps to try to ensure that so far as is practicable:

(a) P is seen in circumstances that would reduce family influences.

---

[169] *ADS v. DSM* [2017] EWCOP 8, in particular at paras 81-82.

(b) The history the person takes and is given is balanced, applied with care and in a way that recognises the difference between fact and assertion.

(c) The explanations, questions and prompts given to P are appropriately framed (e.g. as to why she is expressing the views that she is and what she remembered about relevant parts of her family history).

(d) P should be seen at a neutral venue, having been brought there by someone not involved in the family disputes.

STEP 9 – Case management directions

The Court of Protection will give case management directions leading towards the final hearing of the application. The Court is given very powers to manage a case, and rule 3.7(2) of the Court of Protection Rules 2017 gives a "menu" of directions which the court can give. If any party wishes to apply for a particular direction, then he or she should do so using Form COP9.

Where there is a dispute over whether any person would be entitled to P's estate under the intestacy rules, it may be necessary to consider DNA testing. It has been held that where P lacks capacity to consent to a body sample being taken for DNA testing, the Court of Protection may order that such a sample should be taken.[170]

STEP 10 – The hearing

Hearings in the Court of Protection usually take place either at its central registry at First Avenue House or at one of its regional hearing venues across England and Wales.

170 See *LG v. DK* [2011] EWCOP 2453. See also *Re JC* [2012] COPLR 540 where such a DNA test was carried out, and the terms of an agreed consent order which provides for a DNA test to be carried out are helpfully recorded in the judgment at para 26.

Hearings usually take place in person, although remote hearings have become the default position during the COVID-19 pandemic.[171]

The general rule is that hearings in the Court of Protection will be in private[172], although the Court of Protection may order that a hearing (or part of it) should be held in public.[173] In practice, most hearings take place in public in accordance with Practice Direction 4C, which is entitled "Transparency". This provides that the Court of Protection will ordinarily made an order that any attended hearing[174] shall be in public and, in the same order, impose restrictions in relation to the publication of information about the proceedings.[175] Such an order (known colloquially as a "transparency order") will ordinarily be in the terms of the standard order approved by the President of the Court of Protection and published on the judicial website at https://www.judiciary.gov.uk/publication-court/court-of-protection/ [176]

In most cases[177] the applicant[178] should prepare a bundle and lodge it with the Court of Protection in advance of the hearing in accordance with Practice Direction 4B. The requirements for the bundle are onerous and should be strictly complied with, failing which the court may impose penalties.[179]

---

171 See "Remote Access to the Court of Protection Guidance" issued by Hayden J (the Vice President of the Court of Protection) dated 31 March 2020, available online at https://www.judiciary.uk/wp-content/uploads/2020/04/20200331-Court-of-Protection-Remote-Hearings.pdf

172 Rule 4.1 of the Court of Protection Rules 2017.

173 Rule 4.3 of the Court of Protection Rules 2017.

174 An "attended hearing" is defined as a hearing where one or more of the parties to the proceedings have been invited to attend the court for the determination of the application: see Practice Direction 4C, para 2.2.

175 Practice Direction 4C, para 2.1.

176 Practice Direction 4C, para 2.3.

177 This requirement does not apply to short hearings lasting for less than one hour: see Practice Direction 4B, para 2.1.

178 In some exceptional cases a party other than the applicant may have to prepare the bundle: see Practice Direction 4B, paras 3.1 and 3.2.

179 Practice Direction 4B, para 12.

In *ADS v. DSM*[180] the court stressed the need for the parties to take care in identifying the issues of fact and law raised by the particular case and, to the extent that they are disputed, to consider how such issues can be resolved at the hearing. To the extent that the court is required to conduct a fact finding hearing, it should follow the guidance set out in *AB v. HT*.[181]

Parties should attend the hearing in good time before it is due to start, particularly because this will provide an opportunity to conduct any last minute negotiations. Most hearings take place before a District Judge or the Senior Judge. An authorised court officer cannot hear a statutory will application.[182]

The general format of a hearing is as follows, although the Judge can alter this as he or she deems appropriate:

(1) The applicant (or their legal representative) will introduce the case to the Judge.

(2) The witnesses will then give evidence, with the applicant's witnesses going first followed by each of the other party's witnesses. The general rule is that a witness' witness statement will stand as their evidence[183], and so the party calling that witness need only ask the witness to confirm that the contents of their witness statement are true. It is only if the court gives permission that witnesses can amplify their witness statements or give evidence in relation to new matters which have arisen since the witnesses statement was made.[184] Once each witness has confirmed the truth of their witness statement, the other parties (or their legal representatives) have an opportunity to cross-examine them on their witness statement. It is often the case that

---

180 *ADS v. ASM* [2017] EWCOP 8, in particular at Schedule 2, Part 3.

181 *AB v. HT* [2018] EWCOP 2.

182 Practice Direction 2B, para 2.1.

183 Rule 14.3(2) of the Court of Protection Rules 2017.

184 Rule 14.3(3) of the Court of Protection Rules 2017.

some witnesses give evidence which is uncontentious and so cross examination is unnecessary, and in some cases no cross examination is required at all.

(3) The parties (or their legal representatives) will then make their legal submissions to the Judge.

(4) The Judge then gives judgment. If the Judge authorises the execution of a statutory will, the Judge will make the order at the hearing that authorises the applicant or some other person to execute the statutory will in the terms of an approved draft.

(5) The parties will then address the Judge on costs and any other consequential issues, including any application for permission to appeal. The Judge's ruling on those issues will be included in the order.

STEP 11 – Executing the statutory will

If the Court authorises the execution of a statutory will, it must be executed in accordance with paragraph 3(2) of Schedule 2 to the MCA 2005 which requires that it:

(a) must state that it is signed by P acting by the authorised person,

(b) must be signed by the authorised person with the name of P and his own name, in the presence of two or more witnesses present at the same time,

(c) must be attested and subscribed by those witnesses in the presence of the authorised person, and

(d) must be sealed with the official seal of the Court of Protection.

In ordinary cases, the court order will be drawn up, sealed and copies will be sent to the parties. The statutory will is then executed by the authorised person and witnessed. The applicant must then send the original and two copies of the statutory will back to the Court of

Protection for sealing.[185] The Court of Protection will seal the original and the copy and return both documents to the applicant.[186]

In an emergency case, a statutory will can be engrossed and executed immediately after the order has been made by the judge and before the order has been drawn up and sealed. In such cases it is prudent to ensure for the avoidance of any doubt that the order expressly states that it is effective immediately and without the seal of the court so as to avoid any argument that the statutory will was executed prematurely.

Step 12 – Appeals

The rules on appeals are contained in s.53 of the MCA 2005, Part 20 of the Court of Protection Rules 2017 and Practice Direction 20A. Where an appeal lies to the Court of Appeal, the Civil Procedure Rules apply to such an appeal.[187]

Appeals can generally only be brought with permission of the Court.[188] An application for permission to appeal can be made either to the judge at the original hearing (known as the "first instance judge"), or alternatively to the appeal court.[189] If the first instance judge refuses permission, a further application can be made to the appeal court.[190] The court will only grant permission where it considers that the appeal would have real prospect of success or there is some other compelling reason why the appeal should be heard.[191]

---

185 Practice Direction 9E, para 11.

186 Practice Direction 9E, para 12.

187 Practice Direction 20A, para 1. Part 52 of the Civil Procedure Rules which applies to appeals is available online at www.justice.gov.uk/courts/procedure-rules/civil/rules/part52

188 Rules 20.5 and 20.6 of the Court of Protection Rules 2017.

189 Rule 20.6(2) of the Court of Protection Rules 2017.

190 Rule 20.6(3) of the Court of Protection Rules 2017.

191 Rule 20.8(1) of the Court of Protection Rules 2017.

The rules contain detailed provisions to identify the appropriate appeal court.[192] The rules refer to Tier 1 judges (such as District Judges), Tier 2 judges (such as the Senior Judge) and Tier 3 judges (such as the President of the Court of Protection).[193] The general rule is that an appeal from a Tier 1 judge lies to a Tier 2 judge, an appeal from a Tier 2 judge lies to a Tier 3 judge, and an appeal from a Tier 3 Judge lies to the Court of Appeal. A second appeal (that is, an appeal from a decision of an appeal court) is made to the Court of Appeal.

An appeal is made by filing an appellant's notice on Form COP35[194] and paying the fee which currently stands at £320.[195] Where permission to appeal is sought from the appeal court, it must be applied for in the appellant's notice.[196] The appellants notice must generally be filed within 21 days of the decision being appealed[197], and so anyone considering an appeal must proceed with a degree of urgency. The appeal court will then issue the appellant's notice, and the appellant will then generally have to serve the appellant's notice on the respondents within 21 days of the date on which it was issued.[198]

The appeal hearing is usually limited to a review of the decision of the first instance judge, rather than a re-hearing of the statutory will application itself.[199] The appeal judge will generally not hear any oral evidence or consider any evidence that was not before the first instance

---

192 Rule 20.4 of the Court of Protection Rules 2017.

193 The definitions are contained in rule 2.1 of the Court of Protection Rules 2017.

194 Form COP35 is available online at https://www.gov.uk/government/publications/form-cop35-appellants-notice

195 The application fee is prescribed by the Court of Protection Fees Order 2007, Article 5. Helpful guidance on fees is contained in Form COP44 "Court of Protection fees" which is available online at https://www.gov.uk/government/publications/court-of-protection-fees-cop44

196 Rule 20.10(1) of the Court of Protection Rules 2017.

197 Rule 20.10(2) of the Court of Protection Rules 2017 and Practice Direction 20A, para 4.

198 Rule 20.10(4) of the Court of Protection Rules 2017.

199 Rule 20.14(1) of the Court of Protection Rules 2017.

judge.[200] The appeal judge will only allow an appeal where the decision of the first instance judge was either wrong, or unjust because of a serious procedural or other irregularity in the proceedings before the first instance judge.[201]

---

[200] Rule 20.14(2) of the Court of Protection Rules 2017.

[201] Rule 20.14(3) of the Court of Protection Rules 2017.

CHAPTER SEVEN

HOW DO I MAKE AN URGENT APPLICATION FOR A STATUTORY WILL IN A MEDICAL EMERGENCY?

It is sometimes the case that an application for a statutory will has to be made urgently because there is a real risk that P may die in the very near future. These are perhaps the most difficult cases to deal with in practice. If P does die before the statutory will is authorised then the Court of Protection has no power to authorise a statutory will after P's death.

An urgent application is made using the same procedure as a standard application, as discussed in Chapter 6 of this book, but with the following differences:

(1) The applicant should complete an application form on Form COP9 asking the Court of Protection to deal with the application as a matter of urgency at an expedited hearing.

(2) It is critical that the capacity assessment on Form COP3 and any medical report should address P's diagnosis and life expectancy in detail, and explain why it is feared that P may die imminently. Without such evidence the Court of Protection will not entertain an application for an urgent statutory will.

(3) The COP24 witness statement should explain why the application could not have been made sooner and whether anyone will be prejudiced if the application is heard urgently.

(4) The Official Solicitor and all persons named as respondents to the application should be notified of the application as soon as possible (informally by telephone or email if time does not permit a more formal means of notification), and should be provided

with the application and other documents filed at court, even if only in draft form.

(5) It is prudent to the contact the Court of Protection by telephone or email to notify it that an urgent application is being made. The telephone number is 0300 456 4600. The email address is courtofprotectionenquiries@justice.gov.uk.[202]

The Court of Protection will deal with the case in a way that reflects its urgency, and in extreme cases it will list a hearing with in a matter of days.

Even where there is evidence that P may die imminently, the Court of Protection does not favour urgent applications because they tend to be weighted procedurally in favour of the applicant and could be in breach of Article 6 of the European Convention on Human Rights (the right to a fair trial).[203]

The Court is likely to be particularly concerned to know whether the Official Solicitor and respondents have been notified of the application, whether they have had an opportunity to file evidence in response to the application, and whether they are to be represented at the hearing.

Reported cases involving urgent applications are few and far between, but there are two which shed some light on the Court's approach.

The first is *Re Davey*[204], a striking case where P was a 92 year old lady who had married a 48 year old carer in her nursing home. The marriage automatically revoked P's earlier will which had left her estate to her relatives.[205] The Official Solicitor applied for a statutory will in similar terms to the revoked will, and did so as a matter of urgency given P's age

---

[202] Further information is available at the Court of Protection's website https://www.gov.uk/courts-tribunals/court-of-protection

[203] A statement to this effect was made by Senior Judge Lush in an article entitled "Statutory Wills" in ACTAPS newsletter issue 82 (August 2006).

[204] *Re Davey* [1980] 3 All ER 342; [1981] 1 WLR 164.

[205] By virtue of s.18 of the Wills Act 1837.

and poor health. The application was granted by a deputy master, without notice being given to the husband. That order was upheld on appeal. It was held that the deputy master had properly decided that unreasonable delay would have been caused by ordering the husband to be joined as a party. In reaching this decision the court took into account the fact that the husband could apply for a further statutory will in his favour or, if P died, could make an application for reasonable financial provision out of her estate under the Inheritance (Provision for Family and Dependants) Act 1975.

The second case is *Re R*[206], which is a cautionary tale for anyone contemplating making an urgent application. P was an elderly lady who had made a will in favour of her 2 nephews, A and B, in equal shares. She later made a substantial gift in favour of nephew A, and subsequently lost testamentary capacity. Nephew B became aware of the gift but took no action until 5 years later, when he applied for a statutory will giving himself a legacy of equal value to the gift to Nephew A. The application was made urgently based on a doctor's report that P was terminally ill and would die imminently. Nephew A was notified but did not have time to arrange legal representation at the hearing. The court granted the application, but that decision was overturned on appeal, because it had been impossible to deal fairly with the application at the date of the hearing. The fact that Nephew B had delayed for so long in making the application was a factor which weighed heavily against him.

Where the Court is unwilling to make a final determination of the application because the relevant parties have not been notified or the evidence is incomplete, it may decide to make a so-called "holding will". Such a holding will is a statutory will made on an interim basis to "hold the ring" between the competing arguments until such time as the court is in a position to make a final decision. The Court's power to authorise a holding will is found in section 48 of the MCA 2005, which provides that the Court may make an interim order where:

206 *Re R* [2003] WTLR 1051.

(1) there is reason to believe that P lacks capacity in relation to the matter;

(2) the matter is one to which its powers under the MCA 2005 extend (which is clearly the case in relation to a statutory will: see section 18(1)(i) MCA 2005); and

(3) it is in P's best interests to make an order without delay.

If P dies before the final hearing takes place, then the holding will takes effect in the same way as any other statutory will. The Court will be cautious in deciding on the terms of the holding will and depart from any existing will or the intestacy rules as little as possible. This is in keeping with the principle in section 1(6) of the MCA 2005 that before any act is done or decision is made, regard must be had to whether the purpose for which it is needed can be as effectively achieved in a way that is less restrictive of P's rights and freedom of action.

The Court may authorise a holding will which gives P's residuary estate to a trustees to hold on a discretionary trust. The trustees under such a discretionary trust have the power to distribute the residuary estate among a specified class of potential beneficiaries in such shares as the trustee may determine. A holding will in such terms may be appropriate where it is clear that it would be in P's best interests to include certain persons as beneficiaries but it is not possible to determine what share of the estate each beneficiary should take. It would be prudent for the parties to seek to agree how the trustees might be expected to exercise their powers, and for that agreement to be recorded either in the holding will itself or in an accompanying document.

CHAPTER EIGHT

WHO WILL PAY THE COSTS OF A STATUTORY WILL APPLICATION?

The general rule: costs shall be paid by P or charged to P's estate

The costs of all proceedings in the Court of Protection, including the costs of any statutory will application, are in the discretion of the Court. In other words, the Court has power to choose whether to make a costs order and, if so, in what terms.

The Court's discretion is subject to the Court of Protection Rules 2017 which contain the following general rule concerning proceedings concerning P's property and affairs, which would include any application for a statutory will:

"*Where the proceedings concern P's property and affairs the general rule is that the costs of the proceedings, or that part of the proceedings that concerns P's property and affairs, shall be paid by P or charged to P's estate.*"

Although at first blush this general rule may seem a little hard on P, the rationale which underpins it is that people should not be discouraged by fear of costs penalties from making applications in good faith relating to persons lacking capacity, even if the application is unsuccessful.[207]

This is a fundamentally different approach to other forms of civil litigation, where the starting point is that costs follow the event, or in other words, that the unsuccessful party is ordered to pay the successful party's costs.[208]

---

[207] See *Re Cathcart* [1892] 1 Ch 549.

[208] See the Civil Procedure Rules, rule 44.2(2). This rule is specifically excluded from applying by rule 19.6(5) of the Court of Protection Rules 2017.

Although the general rule is that the costs of a statutory will application will be paid by P or charged to his estate, the Court of Protection can depart from this general rule if the circumstances justify it doing so.[209] In deciding whether departure is justified the court will have regard to all the circumstances including the following specific factors:[210]

(a) The conduct of the parties. This includes:

- conduct before, as well as during, proceedings;
- whether it was reasonable for a party to raise, pursue or contest a particular matter;
- the manner in which a party has made or responded to an application or a particular issue;
- whether a party who has succeeded in that party's application or response to an application, in whole or in part, exaggerated any matter contained in the application or response; and
- any failure by a party to comply with a rule, practice direction or court order;

(b) Whether a party has succeeded on part of that party's case, even if not wholly successful; and

(c) The role of any public body involved in the proceedings.

In practice, the orders made by the Court of Protection during the course of any statutory will application often include a warning to the parties that the Court can depart from the general costs rule set out above. So for example in a recent statutory will case in which the author was involved the Court of Protection made an order which included a recital in the following terms:

> "*The parties are reminded that whilst the usual order for costs in property and affairs cases is that the parties' costs shall be paid from*

[209] Rule 19.5(1) of the Court of Protection Rules 2017.

[210] Rule 19.5(1) and (2) of the Court of Protection Rules 2017.

> *P's funds the court can depart from that position where, for example, a party has unreasonably pursued or contested a particular issue."*

In one case[211] the then Senior Judge of the Court of Protection appeared to go so far as to suggest that the Court should not make a costs order against a party unless they had been given a costs warning of this kind, but that decision was subsequently overruled.[212] It is therefore clear that the Court can make a costs order against a party even if no such warning has been given.

There are no reported cases which specifically deal with the costs of a statutory will application, although one of the textbooks gives some examples which appear to be taken from unreported decisions.[213] There are numerous reported cases on the costs of *other* types of applications regarding P's property and affairs[214], although the Court has repeatedly emphasised that these are essentially no more or less than illustrations of the general rule set out above.[215]

Some particular costs rules

The Court of Protection Rules contain some specific rules which cater for the following particular circumstances:

(1) **Parties with the same interest employing different solicitors** – Where two or more persons having the same interest in relation to a matter act in relation to the proceedings by separate legal representatives, they shall not be permitted more than one set of costs

---

211 See *In the matter of RC; SC v. London Borough of Hackney* [2010] EWCOP B29; [2010] EWHC B29 (COP).

212 See *AH v. Hertfordshire Partnership NHS Foundation Trust* [2011] EWHC 3524 (COP); [2012] COPLR 327.

213 See the Court of Protection Practice 2021 at para 1.858.

214 The key cases are collected and summarised in Heywood & Massey's Court of Protection Practice at 15-015B.

215 See *AH v. Hertfordshire Partnership NHS Foundation Trust*, above, and *JS v. KB and MP (Property and Affairs Deputy for DB)* [2014] EWHC 483 (COP); [2014] COPLR 275.

of the representation unless and to the extent that the court certifies that the circumstances justify separate representation.[216]

Example

Guy has an existing will which leaves his residuary estate to be divided between his 5 children in equal shares. An application is made by Guy's new partner for a statutory will which includes a legacy in her favour. In that scenario the Court is likely to expect the 5 children to instruct a single solicitor. If one child instructs a different solicitor, that child takes the risk that the court may not permit the costs of that different solicitor unless it certifies that the circumstances justify separate representation.

(2) **Litigants in person** – A litigant in person is a party who represents him/herself rather than instructing a solicitor to represent them. A litigant in person is entitled to be reimbursed for their reasonable expenses but is not entitled to claim a fee or remuneration for the time spent by them on the proceedings in the Court of Protection.[217] There is nothing in the Court of Protection Rules or Practice Directions which allows a litigant in person (that is, a person who is representing himself or herself as opposed to instructing a solicitor or barrister to represent them) to recover any sum from P or P's estate or from any other party so as to compensate them for their time spent on the litigation. This is different to other forms of civil litigation where compensation is available.

(3) **The death of P** – The general rule is that where P dies, the Court of Protection's jurisdiction dies with him. But the Court of Protection does retain a residual jurisdiction to deal with certain limited matters

[216] Rule 19.8 of the Court of Protection Rules 2017.

[217] This was the conclusion reached in *Hounslow London Borough v. A Father* [2018] EWCOP 23, noting that neither rule 46.5 of the Civil Procedure Rules nor the Litigants in Person (Costs and Expenses) Act 1975 applies to Court of Protection proceedings.

even after P's death.[218] One of those matters is costs. At any time within 6 years of P's death, the Court of Protection may make an order that costs incurred during P's lifetime be paid out of, or charged to, P's estate.[219]

Example

Samantha makes an application for an order authorising her to execute a statutory will on behalf of her mother, Theresa. Theresa dies unexpectedly, very shortly before the final hearing of the application. Samantha, and the other parties to the application, can seek an order that the costs they have incurred in the application should be paid out of Theresa's estate, provided that the order is made within 6 years of the Theresa's death.

(4) **Wasted costs and costs against third parties** – The Court of Protection has power to make a wasted costs order against a legal representative (such as a solicitor or barrister)[220] or to make a costs order against a third party.[221] These are unusual orders in the context of statutory will applications. If they do arise then reference should be made to the leading textbooks.[222]

The assessment of costs

Whenever the court makes an order about costs which does not provide for fixed costs, then those costs will be subject to assessment. Assessment

[218] See Practice Direction 24B; *Re Joan Treadwell Deceased* [2013] COPLR 587 at para 75 onwards; and *Re A (A Patient now deceased)* [2018] EWCOP 17.

[219] Rule 19.11 of the Court of Protection Rules 2017.

[220] See s.54(4) of the MCA 2005 and rule 19.6 of the Court of Protection Rules 2017, the effect of which is to import the relevant provisions of the Civil Procedure Rules relating to wasted costs, namely rule 46.8 and Practice Direction 46, para 5. See also *Sharma and Judkins v. Hunters* [2011] EWHC 2546 (COP); [2012] COPLR 166.

[221] See rule 19.12(1) of the Court of Protection Rules 2017.

[222] See in particular Heywood and Massey's Court of Protection Practice at 15-015D and 15-017 respectively.

is the procedure by which the Court determines the amount of costs which are payable. Fixed costs are discussed in the next section below.

Costs are assessed on either the standard basis or the indemnity basis.[223] Where the amount of costs is to be assessed on the standard basis, the court will only allow costs which are proportionate to the matters in issue, and will resolve any doubt which it may have as to whether costs were reasonably and proportionately incurred or were reasonable and proportionate in amount in favour of the paying party.[224] In contrast, where the amount of costs is to be assessed on the indemnity basis, there is no requirement of proportionality, and the court will resolve any doubt which it may have as to whether costs were reasonably incurred or were reasonable in amount in favour of the receiving party. In practice, this means that an order that costs are to be assessed on the indemnity basis rather than the standard basis is considerably more favourable to the receiving party.[225] However the court will only award costs on the indemnity basis where the conduct of the parties or other particular circumstances of the case (or both) is such as to take the situation "out of the norm" in a way that justifies an order for indemnity costs.[226]

The assessment itself will be carried out either as a summary assessment or a detailed assessment.

A summary assessment is, as its name suggests, an assessment carried out summarily by the Judge who has heard the application[227], and usually takes place at the conclusion of the hearing. A summary assessment is not generally appropriate where the court orders costs to be paid by P or

---

[223] Rule 44.3(1) of the Civil Procedure Rules.

[224] Rule 44.3(2) of the Civil Procedure Rules.

[225] Rule 44.3(3) of the Civil Procedure Rules.

[226] See *Excelsior Commercial & Industrial Holdings Ltd v. Salisbury Hamer Aspden & Johnson (Costs)* [2002] EWCA Civ 879; [2002] CP Rep 67; *Esure Services Ltd v. Quarcoo* [2009] EWCA Civ 595; and generally the notes in the White Book 2021 at 44.3.8.

[227] See the definition of "summary assessment" in rule 44.1(1) of the Civil Procedure Rules.

charged to P's estate.[228] But where the court orders costs to be paid by anyone other than P, a summary assessment will generally be appropriate if the hearing has lasted for not more than one day.[229] If the hearing disposes of the main application, then the court will summarily assess the costs of the whole application. If the hearing does not dispose of the main application, then the court will summarily assess only the costs of the application or matter to which the hearing related.

A detailed assessment is conducted by way of separate proceedings before the Senior Court Costs Office. The procedure differs depending upon whether the costs are payable by P or charged to P's estate, or whether they are payable by another party.

Where the costs are payable by P or charged to P's estate, the detailed assessment is commenced by filing a request in Form N258B[230] at the Costs Office.[231] This must be done within 3 months after the date when the right to detailed assessment arose.[232] Form N258B sets out a list of documents which must be enclosed with it, together with the fee which currently stands at £85. The Court will direct whether the Form should be served on any other party.[233] Thereafter the Court will provisionally assess the costs and will return the bill to the receiving party.[234] The Court will fix a date for an assessment hearing if the receiving party informs the court, within 14 days after receiving the provisionally assessed bill, that he or she wants the court to hold such a hearing.[235]

---

228 See rule 46.4(2) of the Civil Procedure Rules.

229 See para 9.2 of Practice Direction 44 to the Civil Procedure Rules.

230 The form is available online at https://www.gov.uk/government/publications/form-n258b-request-for-detailed-assessment-costs-payable-out-of-a-fund-other-than-the-community-legal-service-fund

231 Rule 47.19(1) of the Civil Procedure Rules and para 18.3 of Practice Direction 47 to the Civil Procedure Rules.

232 Rule 47.19(2) of the Civil Procedure Rules.

233 Rule 47.19(3) of the Civil Procedure Rules.

234 Rule 47.19(4) and (5) of the Civil Procedure Rules.

235 Rule 47.19(6) of the Civil Procedure Rules.

Where the costs are payable by another party other than P, the detailed assessment is commenced by serving a notice in Form N252[236], together with certain other specified documents, on the paying party.[237] This must be done within 3 months after the event giving rise to the right to detailed assessment, which is generally the making of an order for detailed assessment.[238] The Civil Procedure Rules contained detailed provisions concerning the procedure which should be followed once the notice has been served.[239]

Fixed costs

The Court of Protection may permit a party to recover their fixed costs in accordance with Practice Direction 19B. That Practice Direction applies where professional deputies are entitled to recover costs out of P's estate. The fixed costs prescribed by the Practice Direction are limited to certain specific court applications and non-contentious work, none of which concerns statutory wills. In practice, therefore, fixed costs do not generally apply in statutory will applications.

Appeals on costs

In theory costs orders, like any other court orders, can be subject to an appeal.[240] In practice, however, costs appeals are notoriously difficult "*because the trial judge has a wide discretion with the result that [the appeal] court will only interfere with his decision if he has exceeded the generous ambit within which there is usually much room for reasonable disagreement*

---

236 The form is available online at https://assets.publishing.service.gov.uk/government/uploads/attachment_data/file/688564/n252-ang.pdf

237 Rule 5.2 of Practice Direction 47 to the Civil Procedure Rules.

238 Rule 47.7 of the Civil Procedure Rules.

239 See rules 47.6 to 47.17 of the Civil Procedure Rules, Practice Direction 47 to the Civil Procedure Rules and the Practice Note issued by the Senior Costs Judge in July 2020 entitled "Hearings and Detailed Assessments in the Senior Courts Costs Office", a copy of which is available online.

240 The procedure for appeals is discussed in Chapter 6 of this book.

or because, even more unusually, he has erred in principle".[241] The costs of any appeal will be governed by the Civil Procedure Rules rather than the Court of Protection Rules.

[241] See *Re G (An Adult) (by her litigation friend, the Official Solicitor) (Costs)* [2015] EWCA Civ 446; [2015] COPLR 438, at para 22.

CHAPTER NINE

WHAT IS THE NATURE AND EFFECT OF A STATUTORY WILL?

The nature and effect of a statutory will is set out in paragraph 4 of Schedule 2 to the MCA 2005 which insofar as it is relevant provides as follows:

> "*Wills: effect of execution*
>
> *4 (1) This paragraph applies where a will is executed in accordance with paragraph 3.*[242]
>
> *(2) The Wills Act 1837 (c.26) has effect in relation to the will as if it were signed by P by his own hand, except that –*
>
> *(a) section 9 of the 1837 Act (requirements as to signing and attestation) does not apply, and*
>
> *(b) in the subsequent provisions of the 1837 Act any reference to execution in the manner required by the previous provisions is to be read as a reference to execution in accordance with paragraph 3.*
>
> *(3) The will has the same effect for all purposes as if –*
>
> *(a) P had had the capacity to make a valid will, and*
>
> *(b) the will had been executed by him in the manner required by the 1837 Act...*"

The effect of this provision is that the only difference between a statutory will and any other kind of will is how it is signed and witnessed. The rules about how a statutory will should be signed and witnessed are set out in

[242] The execution of a statutory will in accordance with para 3 of Schedule 2 to the MCA 2005 is discussed in the last part of Chapter 6 of this book.

paragraph 3 of Schedule 2 to the MCA 2005 and have been discussed in Chapter 6 of this book. If those rules are followed, then the statutory will takes effect in the same way as any other valid will.

The effect of a statutory will which involves an international element is discussed in Chapter 5 of this book.

The question arises whether a person who is disappointed with what (if anything) they stand to receive under a statutory will could bring a claim after P's death to challenge the validity of the statutory will. In relation to ordinary, non-statutory wills, such claims – which are known as contentious probate claims – are not uncommon. Challenges are typically brought on the grounds that the will was not properly executed[243], or that the deceased lacked testamentary capacity[244], did not know and approve of the will[245], or was subject to undue influence[246]. In relation to a statutory will, however, the effect of paragraph 4(3) of Schedule 2 to the MCA 2005, quoted above, is that P will be deemed to have testamentary capacity and to have executed the statutory will in accordance with the formalities required by the Wills Act 1837. In practice this means that it would be impossible for anyone to bring a claim after P's death to challenge the validity statutory will on the ground that P lacked capacity or that the statutory will did not comply with the formalities required by the Wills Act 1837. Furthermore, given that the court has authorised the execution of the statutory will on behalf of P, it would be very difficult if not impossible to argue that P did not know and approve of the statutory will or that he was subject to undue influence.[247]

[243] See, for example, *Gardiner v. Tabet* [2021] EWHC 563 (Ch) where it was alleged that someone other than the deceased signed the disputed will.

[244] See, for example, *Re Burns deceased* [2016] EWCA Civ 137 where the Court of Appeal upheld the validity of a will made by a elderly lady notwithstanding that she was showing signs of mental impairment.

[245] See, for example, *Gill v. Woodall* [2010] EWCA Civ 1430; [2011] Ch 380 where the Court of Appeal reviewed the law on lack of knowledge and approval.

[246] The law on undue influence in the context of wills is summarised in *Edwards v. Edwards* [2007] EWHC 1119 (Ch); [2007] WTLR 1387 at para 47.

[247] Save perhaps where there is fraud in connection with the proceedings before the court, as suggested in Heywood & Massey's Court of Protection Practice at 20-054.

A statutory will could, however, be subject to other claims after P's death. For example:

(1) If a will fails to make reasonable financial provision for certain categories of person (namely spouse, civil partner, former spouse, child, a person treated as a child, cohabitant and dependant), then they may apply for reasonable financial provision under the Inheritance (Provision for Family and Dependants) Act 1975 ("the 1975 Act").[248] In principle there is no reason why a claim under the 1975 Act could not be made in respect of a statutory will. Claims under the 1975 Act by anyone other than a spouse or civil partner are limited to maintenance[249], and so if such a claimant has sufficient financial resources to maintain themselves to a reasonable standard then they are unlikely to have a claim.[250] Claims by a spouse or civil partner are not so limited but instead extend to whatever is reasonable for them to receive in all the circumstances.[251]

(2) If P promised to leave certain property in his will to a person who then relied upon that promise to their detriment, then that person may have a proprietary estoppel claim against the estate.[252] There is no reason in principle why such a claim should not be pursued even where the court has authorised a statutory will on behalf of P.

---

[248] The leading case on 1975 Act claims is the Supreme Court's decision in *Ilott v. Blue Cross* [2018] AC 545.

[249] See section 1(2)(b) of the 1975 Act.

[250] In *Espinosa v. Bourke* [1999] 1 FLR 747, 752, which involved a 1975 Act claim by an adult child, the Court of Appeal stated that: "*The financial position of the applicant may determine the application. However rich the deceased, if the applicant has sufficient financial resources and no financial needs, it would not be necessary for the court to look further*".

[251] See section 1(2)(a) of the 1975 Act; and *Lilleyman v. Lilleyman* [2012] EWHC 821 (Ch); [2013] Ch 825.

[252] See *Davies v. Davies* [2016] EWCA Civ 463; [2017] 1 FLR 1286 where the essential principles of proprietary estoppel are summarised at para. 38.

(3) In the unlikely event that the meaning of the statutory will is disputed, then a claim could be brought for the court to determine its meaning[253] or even for the statutory will to be rectified[254], although in practice such claims are rare.

There is likewise no reason in principle why a statutory will could not be subject to a variation, that is, a direction from a beneficiary to the personal representatives to transfer property to someone other than the original beneficiary. Such variations are common in practice. If they are carried out within 2 years of P's death and comply with the other requirements of section 142 of the Inheritance Tax Act 1984 then the variation will take effect as if it were contained in the statutory will, which can have beneficial tax consequences.

Example

The Court of Protection authorises a statutory will to be made on behalf of Paul which leaves his estate to his wife and children. After Paul dies it transpires that he had a son, John, by a previous relationship, although nobody (including the Judge in the Court of Protection) knew anything about this. John is upset that he was left nothing in the statutory will. He is advised that there are no grounds for challenging the validity of the statutory will, and that, although he is eligible to bring a 1975 Act claim, any such claim is unlikely to succeed because he has sufficient resources to maintain himself. John approaches Paul's wife who agrees to give him a legacy. Solicitors are instructed who prepare a Deed of Variation, the effect of which is that the legacy is treated as if it were contained in the statutory will.

[253] See *Wesley v. Chanter* [2018] EWHC 21 (Ch) where the High Court consider how a statutory codicil should be interpreted.

[254] The court's jurisdiction to rectify a will is contained in section 20 of the Administration of Justice Act 1982, as discussed by the Supreme Court in *Marley v. Rawlings* [2014] UKSC 2; [2015] AC 129.

CHAPTER TEN

CAN I NEGOTIATE A COMPROMISE OF A STATUTORY WILL APPLICATION OUT OF COURT?

It is possible for the parties involved in a statutory will application to negotiate a compromise of that application, although if that compromise involves the execution of a statutory will (or the withdrawal of any ongoing proceedings) then the Court of Protection will need to approve the compromise and, if appropriate, authorise the execution of the statutory will on P's behalf. The Court will only do so if it considers that it would be in P's best interests.

Many applications are resolved amicably in this way and compromise is to be encouraged. In *ADS v. DSM*[255] the court suggested that consideration of whether the application could have proceeded on an uncontested basis was sensible.[256] The same case also indicates that the court will generally give great weight to the compromise agreement in determining whether a statutory will should be authorised on P's behalf.

The parties are free to negotiate in any way they choose, and often do so either in direct conversations between themselves or in correspondence. Before conducting any negotiations about a statutory will, the parties must ensure that there is evidence that rebuts the presumption that P has testamentary capacity, and that they have taken steps to ascertain P's wishes and feelings so far as it possible so that they can be considered during the negotiations.

Negotiations can be carried out in one of three ways:

---

[255] [2017] COPLR 231.

[256] See paras 2 to 4 of Part 2 of Schedule 2 to the judgment.

(1) On an "open" basis – which means that the parties are free to tell the court about the negotiations at any subsequent hearing.

(2) On a "without prejudice" basis – which means that the court must not be told about the negotiations at all.

(3) On a "without prejudice save as to costs" basis – which means that the court can only be told about the negotiations when the court comes to decide costs.

Where a party unreasonably refuses another party's offer which is made on either an "open" basis or a "without prejudice save as to costs" basis, then that amounts to conduct which the court can take into account in deciding whether the depart from the general rule that the costs of the statutory will application will be paid by P or charged to P's estate.[257]

The Court of Protection Rules do not contain any equivalent of the Part 36 offer under the Civil Procedure Rules.[258]

There are two methods of negotiation which deserve particular mention. The first is a best interests meeting, which is a formal meeting attended by all relevant parties, usually held on an "open" basis, at which the parties seek to agree on what decision should be taken in P's best interests. Such meetings are common in health and welfare cases, particularly those involving local authorities and other public bodies, but are less frequently encountered in property and affairs cases, and are rare in statutory will applications.

Secondly there is mediation. Mediation is a common form of negotiation in other forms of civil litigation, and is becoming increasingly popular in Court of Protection cases. Mediation is a voluntary process in which the parties agree to instruct a mediator to facilitate the resolution of their dispute. The mediator is an independent third party, who is usually a

---

[257] Costs are discussed in Chapter 8 of this book.

[258] A Part 36 offer under the Civil Procedure Rules is one which, if it is not accepted by the other side but is beaten at trial, has automatic costs consequences which are highly favourable to the offeror. See https://www.justice.gov.uk/courts/procedure-rules/civil/rules/part36

barrister or solicitor. The mediation takes place either "in person" at an agreed venue, or remotely via an online platform such as Zoom. It will be up to the parties to reach an agreement, with the mediator shuttling between them to facilitate communication, to promote understanding, to focus the parties on the key issues and to encourage creative problem solving.

Since 1 October 2019 a nationwide pilot mediation scheme has been running to facilitate and evaluate mediation in the Court of Protection. Full details of the scheme are available online at https://www.courtofprotectionmediation.uk. The scheme has certain particular features as follows:

(1) The scheme is only available for disputes which have resulted in proceedings being issued in the Court of Protection.

(2) The scheme includes a panel of expert mediators who are willing to work at the legal aid rate of £100.80 per hour plus travel costs.

(3) The parties and the mediator are obliged to consider how P can participate in the mediation.

(4) The scheme helpfully includes various proforma documents to assist the parties, including a draft agreement to mediate, a mediation questionnaire for participants, checklists for parties and the mediator, and a draft mediation settlement agreement.

(5) Mediations conducted under the scheme are confidentially evaluated by a team led by Dr Jaime Lindsey of the University of Essex. When the parties appoint the mediator under the scheme they will be asked to consent to their contact details being provided to the evaluation team. The findings of the evaluation will be published in a freely available report in due course.

MORE BOOKS BY LAW BRIEF PUBLISHING

'Covid-19, Homeworking and the Law – The Essential Guide to Employment and GDPR Issues' by Forbes Solicitors
'Covid-19, Force Majeure and Frustration of Contracts – The Essential Guide' by Keith Markham
'Covid-19 and Criminal Law – The Essential Guide' by Ramya Nagesh
'Covid-19 and Family Law in England and Wales – The Essential Guide' by Safda Mahmood
'A Practical Guide to the Law of Unlawful Eviction and Harassment – 2nd Edition' by Stephanie Lovegrove
'Covid-19, Residential Property, Equity Release and Enfranchisement – The Essential Guide' by Paul Sams and Louise Uphill
'Covid-19, Brexit and the Law of Commercial Leases – The Essential Guide' by Mark Shelton
'A Practical Guide to Costs in Personal Injury Claims – 2nd Edition' by Matthew Hoe
'A Practical Guide to the General Data Protection Regulation (GDPR) – 2nd Edition' by Keith Markham
'Ellis on Credit Hire – Sixth Edition' by Aidan Ellis & Tim Kevan
'A Practical Guide to Working with Litigants in Person and McKenzie Friends in Family Cases' by Stuart Barlow
'Protecting Unregistered Brands: A Practical Guide to the Law of Passing Off' by Lorna Brazell
'A Practical Guide to Secondary Liability and Joint Enterprise Post-Jogee' by Joanne Cecil & James Mehigan
'A Practical Guide to the Pre-Action RTA Claims Protocol for Personal Injury Lawyers' by Antonia Ford
'A Practical Guide to Neighbour Disputes and the Law' by Alexander Walsh
'A Practical Guide to Forfeiture of Leases' by Mark Shelton
'A Practical Guide to Coercive Control for Legal Practitioners and Victims' by Rachel Horman

'A Practical Guide to Rights Over Airspace and Subsoil' by Daniel Gatty
'Tackling Disclosure in the Criminal Courts – A Practitioner's Guide' by Narita Bahra QC & Don Ramble
'A Practical Guide to the Law of Driverless Cars – Second Edition' by Alex Glassbrook, Emma Northey & Scarlett Milligan
'A Practical Guide to TOLATA Claims' by Greg Williams
'Artificial Intelligence – The Practical Legal Issues' by John Buyers
'A Practical Guide to the Law of Prescription in Scotland' by Andrew Foyle
'A Practical Guide to the Construction and Rectification of Wills and Trust Instruments' by Edward Hewitt
'A Practical Guide to the Law of Bullying and Harassment in the Workplace' by Philip Hyland
'How to Be a Freelance Solicitor: A Practical Guide to the SRA-Regulated Freelance Solicitor Model' by Paul Bennett
'A Practical Guide to Prison Injury Claims' by Malcolm Johnson
'A Practical Guide to the Small Claims Track' by Dominic Bright
'A Practical Guide to Advising Clients at the Police Station' by Colin Stephen McKeown-Beaumont
'A Practical Guide to Antisocial Behaviour Injunctions' by Iain Wightwick
'Practical Mediation: A Guide for Mediators, Advocates, Advisers, Lawyers, and Students in Civil, Commercial, Business, Property, Workplace, and Employment Cases' by Jonathan Dingle with John Sephton
'The Mini-Pupillage Workbook' by David Boyle
'A Practical Guide to Crofting Law' by Brian Inkster
'A Practical Guide to Spousal Maintenance' by Liz Cowell
'A Practical Guide to the Law of Domain Names and Cybersquatting' by Andrew Clemson
'A Practical Guide to the Law of Gender Pay Gap Reporting' by Harini Iyengar

'A Practical Guide to the Rights of Grandparents in Children Proceedings' by Stuart Barlow
'NHS Whistleblowing and the Law' by Joseph England
'Employment Law and the Gig Economy' by Nigel Mackay & Annie Powell
'A Practical Guide to Noise Induced Hearing Loss (NIHL) Claims' by Andrew Mckie, Ian Skeate, Gareth McAloon
'An Introduction to Beauty Negligence Claims – A Practical Guide for the Personal Injury Practitioner' by Greg Almond
'Intercompany Agreements for Transfer Pricing Compliance' by Paul Sutton
'Zen and the Art of Mediation' by Martin Plowman
'A Practical Guide to the SRA Principles, Individual and Law Firm Codes of Conduct 2019 – What Every Law Firm Needs to Know' by Paul Bennett
'A Practical Guide to Adoption for Family Lawyers' by Graham Pegg
'A Practical Guide to Industrial Disease Claims' by Andrew Mckie & Ian Skeate
'A Practical Guide to Redundancy' by Philip Hyland
'A Practical Guide to Vicarious Liability' by Mariel Irvine
'A Practical Guide to Applications for Landlord's Consent and Variation of Leases' by Mark Shelton
'A Practical Guide to Relief from Sanctions Post-Mitchell and Denton' by Peter Causton
'A Practical Guide to Equity Release for Advisors' by Paul Sams
'A Practical Guide to the Law Relating to Food' by Ian Thomas
'A Practical Guide to Financial Services Claims' by Chris Hegarty
'The Law of Houses in Multiple Occupation: A Practical Guide to HMO Proceedings' by Julian Hunt
'A Practical Guide to Unlawful Eviction and Harassment' by Stephanie Lovegrove
'Occupiers, Highways and Defective Premises Claims: A Practical Guide Post-Jackson – 2nd Edition' by Andrew Mckie

'A Practical Guide to Financial Ombudsman Service Claims' by Adam Temple & Robert Scrivenor
'A Practical Guide to Advising Schools on Employment Law' by Jonathan Holden
'A Practical Guide to Running Housing Disrepair and Cavity Wall Claims: 2nd Edition' by Andrew Mckie & Ian Skeate
'A Practical Guide to Holiday Sickness Claims – 2nd Edition' by Andrew Mckie & Ian Skeate
'Arguments and Tactics for Personal Injury and Clinical Negligence Claims' by Dorian Williams
'A Practical Guide to Drone Law' by Rufus Ballaster, Andrew Firman, Eleanor Clot
'A Practical Guide to Compliance for Personal Injury Firms Working With Claims Management Companies' by Paul Bennett
'A Practical Guide to Dog Law for Owners and Others' by Andrea Pitt
'RTA Allegations of Fraud in a Post-Jackson Era: The Handbook – 2nd Edition' by Andrew Mckie
'RTA Personal Injury Claims: A Practical Guide Post-Jackson' by Andrew Mckie
'On Experts: CPR35 for Lawyers and Experts' by David Boyle
'An Introduction to Personal Injury Law' by David Boyle
'A Practical Guide to Subtle Brain Injury Claims' by Pankaj Madan

These books and more are available to order online direct from the publisher at www.lawbriefpublishing.com, where you can also read free sample chapters. For any queries, contact us on 0844 587 2383 or mail@lawbriefpublishing.com.

Our books are also usually in stock at www.amazon.co.uk with free next day delivery for Prime members, and at good legal bookshops such as Wildy & Sons.

We are regularly launching new books in our series of practical day-to-day practitioners' guides. Visit our website and join our free newsletter to be kept informed and to receive special offers, free chapters, etc.

You can also follow us on Twitter at www.twitter.com/lawbriefpub.

www.ingramcontent.com/pod-product-compliance
Ingram Content Group UK Ltd.
Pitfield, Milton Keynes, MK11 3LW, UK
UKHW021239300926
15471UKWH00013B/771

9 781913 715724